T0098694

At my university, the band definitely marched to its own drummer and that band was the best part of college for me. It's no wonder then that I've gravitated to Patti and Milledge's vision of retirement (or anti-retirement, as they would say). Their view of the postcareer stage of life as a time when you can not only follow your own drummer but be your own drummer is exactly how I want to live. This book provides a map for getting there, whether you are already retired or just thinking about it. In fact, I've already begun considering some of the resolutions. When the time comes to bid my career goodbye, I'll be ready, thanks to The Resolutionist.

–David Banner, CEO, actor, producer, and artist

This is a tale of profound importance. Hundreds of thousands of Americans at the ends of impressive careers aren't fading into quiet irrelevance. They're taking on community tasks, building organizations, recovering old dreams, discovering new passions, and doing good while doing well; my guess is that they will save the arts, the parks, and the topmost colleges. Are these newly self-aware and often youthful elders alive to visions as large as their remarkable capacities? Will we find among them agents for the social and environmental changes we so urgently require? The Harts have given us much to ponder.

–Bruce Payne, lecturer, Hunter College (CUNY)

If you are looking for a guide to what your postcareer life could look like, you have found it. I have had the incredible good fortune to see Patti and Milledge negotiate these questions over the last twenty years. They have distilled their lessons into a readable, engaging blueprint for figuring out what's next. Most importantly, this is not some theory. I see how they consistently turn their anti-retirement words into resolute actions. They seem happier and more engaged, and they are having more impact than they ever have. And they're doing it on purpose. If you're asking these kinds of questions, you should read this book.

–Buddy Teaster, CEO of Soles4Souls and author of *Shoestrings*

PATTI & MILLEDGE HART

THE RESØLUTIONIST

WELCOME
TO THE
ANTI-RETIREMENT
MOVEMENT

Advantage®

Published by Advantage, Charleston, South Carolina.
Member of Advantage Media Group.

ADVANTAGE is a registered trademark, and the Advantage colophon is a trademark of Advantage Media Group, Inc.

Printed in the United States of America.

10 9 8 7 6 5 4 3 2 1

ISBN: 978-1-64225-124-1
LCCN: 2020921319

Cover design by David Taylor.
Layout design by Wesley Strickland.

This publication is designed to provide accurate and authoritative information in regard to the subject matter covered. It is sold with the understanding that the publisher is not engaged in rendering legal, accounting, or other professional services. If legal advice or other expert assistance is required, the services of a competent professional person should be sought.

Advantage Media Group is proud to be a part of the Tree Neutral® program. Tree Neutral offsets the number of trees consumed in the production and printing of this book by taking proactive steps such as planting trees in direct proportion to the number of trees used to print books. To learn more about Tree Neutral, please visit www.treeneutral.com.

Advantage Media Group is a publisher of business, self-improvement, and professional development books and online learning. We help entrepreneurs, business leaders, and professionals share their Stories, Passion, and Knowledge to help others Learn & Grow. Do you have a manuscript or book idea that you would like us to consider for publishing? Please visit advantagefamily.com or call 1.866.775.1696.

We dedicate this to our grandmothers,
Georgia Gleason and Ruby Neil Hart, for the
groundbreaking way they lived their lives and
their continuing influence on ours.

CONTENTS

FOREWORD

IF BEFORE THE onset of COVID-19 I had written this foreword urging retirement-age individuals to forget completely about welcoming an essentially passive retirement for themselves, and choose instead to embrace an entirely new, energetic stage of active life centering on pursuing their lifelong passions, any right-minded individuals might reasonably have rejected such an improbable course of action as sheer insanity. Having yearned for years to reach the eligibility for retirement and the leisurely life they picture as characterizing it, why would any sane individual now reject the anticipated years of a reward which their work had earned them?

However, if my own experience is any guide, having been subjected to several recent months of the confining burdens of "lockdown," "sheltering in place," and "social distancing," many thoughtful individuals are more likely today to welcome and embrace with relief and enthusiasm an entirely new, energetic phase of their lives that would be exactly the opposite of the enforced boredom often resulting from COVID-19's constraints. Moreover, such a life could accurately be characterized as indeed just the opposite of retirement—a new kind of purposeful active engagement with their lifelong passions, a golden opportunity to sink their teeth into the psychically rewarding challenges of making a difference in their life and/or world for the better, and/or to develop at least some of their innate but as yet undeveloped talents or interests into self-fulfilling, self-satisfying, and society-benefiting achievements. In this new age in which more and more thoughtful Americans of every generation are yearning for fresh, unifying, moderate public leadership, perhaps you would find great psychic satisfaction in pouring your time, energy, and ideas even into public service.

Fortunately for all of us who didn't need to experience the isolation required by COVID-19 to foresee what our imagined retirement life would be like, the richly experienced "power couple" Milledge and Patti Hart foresaw the opportunities open to all who have lived and enjoyed a highly successful life of work and achievement as a practical, appealing, and challenging follow-on life as a real alternative to retirement. Both Milledge and Patti separately achieved important roles in their respective professional careers—Patti in the corporate world and Milledge in investment banking, launching start-ups, and management—and had tasted the joy and fulfillment of their unremittingly energetic lives. Neither of them felt fatigued or exhausted by the exertions required by their active professional roles. Indeed, just the opposite. They had tasted the joy of energetic engagement in fulfilling the responsibilities of those roles and came to realize how greatly they thrived in those pursuits. It was that realization that drew them to choosing to devote the heart of their "postwork" lives to equally energetic pursuit of achieving distinction—making a difference for themselves and for society—in goals that they personally care deeply about.

The big difference that drove their choice was this: their professional lives were devoted to achieving missions given to them by the corporations or clients with whom they worked. In choosing to become "resolutionists" they would be pouring their later lives into achieving the pursuits they personally chose themselves. Both Milledge and Patti understand that to follow their vision requires personal resolve, and that is why they chose to call those who join in their movement "resolutionists." It is the satisfaction of resolving to devote all of their energies to personally chosen pursuits or to the fulfillment of realizing and polishing their own interests, talents, and long-postponed fascinations that would make their lives as "resolutionists" more appealing than the passive retirement activities that many "retirees" choose simply to fill the time that is weighing heavily on their hands.

Each of the Harts had succeeded impressively in their separate careers for around forty years and, on reflection, came to the conclusion that they wanted more challenges still, but indeed different kinds of challenges and fulfillment from their postwork stages of life than any conventional picture of retirement would ever have provided them. In their book *The Resolutionist: Welcome to the Anti-Retirement Movement*, they have provided for all of us a book of personally tested strategies on how to visualize, commence, and orchestrate an active and rewarding postwork life for each of us.

Once you try out the challenge of embracing some of these strategies, I predict that you, too, will embrace your new lives as "resolutionists," and you will thank Milledge and Patti Hart for enabling you to learn new joys from their own lives' experience!

–Joel L. Fleishman
  Professor of Law and Public Policy, Duke University
  Author of *Putting Wealth to Work: Philanthropy for Today or Investing for Tomorrow (New York: PublicAffairs Books, 2017)*

ACKNOWLEDGMENTS

THANKS TO ALL of our fellow Resolutionists for contributing their stories to this book and for providing us with the moral and emotional support required to take the leap to this stage of life. We would also like to recognize the many "groundbreakers" that have refused to allow social norms to define them and their lifestyle…we are inspired by your courage. To our son, Dustin, who made all the trials and tribulations of our work life worth it. Now we have you and your husband, Jon, in our lives to make everything so much more interesting. And, to our families, thank you for supporting us even when the paths we chose were not expected.

THE 12 RESOLUTIONS

1. **RIP THE BAND-AID OFF**: Create a dramatic change from your working life.

2. **GET COMFORTABLE WITH THE UNCOMFORTABLE**: Force yourself to move outside of your comfort zone—do something new!

3. **PRIORITIZE YOURSELF**: For the first time, you can be the priority—your interests, your passions, your health and wellness.

4. **BE YOUR OWN BEST FRIEND**: At this new stage, you will often find that the things you are most interested in are yours alone—have the courage to fly solo.

5. **FIND YOUR PASSION**: In many cases our passions were set aside during our working lives. Now let them come to the surface—and welcome them into this stage of life.

6. **DEVELOP YOUR ELEVATOR PITCH**: Create a story for what you are doing today. Your current life is engaging and interesting—let others know!

7. **ENGAGE YOUR RESOURCES:** You have built a treasure trove of resources: wisdom, experience, personal network, wealth, successes, and failures. Utilize your past to enhance your future.

8. **DREAM LESS AND DO MORE:** Tackle the list of things that you have always wanted to do. Whatever has been on your list of "dreams" move to your action list!

9. **LEVERAGE YOUR SUCCESS:** Use what you have earned and learned to become a happy Resolutionist!

10. **SURROUND YOURSELF WITH KINDRED SPIRITS:** This is the time in life to embrace those who are supportive of your journey.

11. **DEVELOP A NEW METRIC SYSTEM:** Find new ways to define "winning."

12. **SAY GOODBYE TO FOMO:** Stay focused on your dreams and passions by overcoming the "fear of missing out."

PART I:

SETTING THE STAGE

I want every stage of my life to be more exciting than the last.

—Madeleine Albright

NOT LONG AGO Willard Scott of the *Today* show hosted a weekly segment where he wished viewers who were a hundred years old or older a happy birthday. Hitting the "one hundred" milestone was a rarity, and it certainly felt like national TV congratulations, complete with a picture, were in order. Although Willard Scott has retired, the *Today* show still runs that feature, but it's just not the same. Today we all know people who are active well into their nineties, and envisioning them reaching the century mark isn't farfetched—or all that newsworthy.

PATTI

For the first two-thirds of my career, I was the first woman ... fill in the blank. The first woman director. The first woman vice president. The first woman in a corporate boardroom for whatever company I was serving. The first woman to win a specific award. I was fortunate to be a member of the inaugural *Fortune* magazine "50 Most Powerful Women" issue. So it was the first, the first, the first—and then things changed. During the last five years of my career, I would look around a room and see many talented women. Almost without me noticing, the ratio had changed from having just one woman in the room or on the board to having significant numbers. It was a much more comfortable situation, and it wouldn't have happened if these women hadn't pushed for change. They defied social norms, redesigned long-serving models, and broke all of the molds that constrained the women before them. No one knew it then, but they embodied the Resolutionist spirit. *They not only embraced change—they initiated change.*

When I began thinking about leaving my hard-driving (and hard-won!) career behind, I realized I didn't want to take on a traditional retirement life any more than I had wanted to take on a traditional "female" career forty years ago. I observed those that had gone before me and knew that I wanted more. I didn't want to stop learning, growing, challenging myself. But there was no defined path for what I wanted to do. So I said to myself, "Patti, you'll just have to be the first again. You've done it before. You can do it again." I wanted to keep the change momentum going into my postcareer life, to establish a movement of anti-retirement comrades and to label them Resolutionists. And that is exactly what I'm doing now.

According to the Stanford Longevity Center, the perception that more people are living to see their hundredth birthday is firmly based in reality. In fact, in less than a century, average life expectancy in the developed world has increased about thirty years.[1]

What does this mean for you? It means you will have a lot of postcareer years to fill. It means you could spend nearly as many years in the "retirement" phase of your life as you did in the career phase. It means that postcareer planning, which has traditionally been focused on making sure you didn't run out of money, needs to be replaced by longevity planning, which focuses on what you will do with all that time.

So what will you do? Most of us have spent a long time making sure we are financially ready to retire, but what will you do with your time? How do you envision your days? How do you know that you will be happy and fulfilled?

How we plan for retirement is dictated by what we think retirement *means. Is retirement a fading away, or is it a time to engage in passions? Is it a time of quiet or a time of new challenges? Is it a time to watch pennies or a time to travel?* To obtain a better understanding of how people visualize the years after they have stepped away from full-time employment, researchers at the MIT AgeLab asked participants to provide five words for how they imagined their "life

---

1   Stanford Center on Longevity, http://longevity.stanford.edu/about-the-center/.

after career."[2] Turns out people don't have a very clear or deep view of their postcareer life. Just twenty-eight words accounted for half of all responses received. Some of those words have distinctly negative connotations—*death, old, boring, tired, lonely*—but others were more hopeful. *Happy, relax, travel, fun, enjoy, family*, and *freedom* were often used to describe retirement. Less often cited were words such as *peace, calm, content, time, rest*, and *easy*. Even further down the list were *exciting* and *adventure*. None of these responses are surprising in themselves, but when taken together, they present a very small and insular postcareer world.

MILLEDGE

I would never call myself retired. I'm busier now than I've ever been. And contrary to the stereotype of retirement, I'm learning more, contributing more, and growing more than I ever did when my days were spent managing companies or growing an investment bank from the ground up. I'm a planner and goal setter by nature. These traits served me well in the world of finance, where team members, clients, and investors depended on my decisions. They were particularly helpful when I was serving as the CEO at four different companies during a time of acquisition, restructuring, growth, and ultimately selling each of them. But I also like to think of myself as someone who is never satisfied with the status quo. I want to always be doing something new. Meeting new people. Taking

---

2   "The Longevity Economy," AgeLab, accessed September 29, 2020, https://agelab.mit.edu/longevity-economy.

on a new hobby. Reading a new book that makes me view the world in a different way. Challenging myself. I never thought I'd retire because I thought retirement meant slowing down. What I've found is that I'm not retired. I'm a Resolutionist. I'm using this time to be a better me than I could when my days were structured and my time was spoken for. And once I embraced the new me, I found there are an awful lot of others out there who are changing the perception of retirement and making it a time to look forward to. Not because it's a time to relax—though I do plenty of that—but because it is a time to explore, be adventurous, and be the person you always wanted to be. Being a Resolutionist is exactly what I wanted to be—even if I didn't know it until I was deep into the postcareer phase of life.

Writing about the study in his book *The Longevity Economy*, the AgeLab's director, Joseph F. Coughlin, observed, "There are *parrots* with larger vocabularies than most of us have concerning life in old age."[3]

The generation reaching retirement age today, however, has always had a lot to say, and the fact that we are entering a postcareer stage is unlikely to change that behavior. The concept of "retirement" being a time when everyone slows down and takes a back seat to what is happening around us is fast becoming outdated, as this generation consistently defies norms. It's a cohort that has changed cultural, social,

---

3   *The Longevity Economy: Unlocking the World's Fastest-Growing, Most Misunderstood Market*, Joseph F. Coughlin, 2017.

and corporate mores during their time in the workforce, and we see no reason to accept an outdated narrative of later life. Instead, we look forward to these years as Resolutionists who continue to live a fulfilled and interesting life.

Reaching "retirement age" once meant leaving the workforce to pursue leisure activities, but today's aging population is reinventing life after sixty-five. More than 20 percent are continuing to work,[4] some because they need to but many more because they like their work and their self-worth is tied up in it. Still others are finding this a time to follow their passions and lead a fulfilling

Retirement is no longer a story of old age. It is a story of long life. It's the story of the anti-retirement movement!

life on their own terms. And there is no reason you can't do it all—work longer, then step back to follow your passions, then step back further to relax—just at different times. Retirement is no longer a story of old age. It is a story of long life. It's the story of the anti-retirement movement!

Being anti-retirement doesn't mean we intend to keep working at a full-time career (though we will if we want to). It means we are changing how we live in this postcareer life. We are stepping into the next phase as Resolutionists, who are changing the model for ourselves and those who follow. We are resolving to do it our way. We are resolving to make these years just as productive as our career years, if not more so.

But it isn't always easy. During your career you had structure, goals, and people who relied on you and made you feel important.

---

4   "More Americans Working Past 65," AARP, April 2019.

When you leave your career, it is up to you to find your own path, develop your own structure, and find new ways to measure success. This book will help you find your way. We've already worked our way through many of the roadblocks and around the stumbling stones and down the dead-end paths. And we've found twelve resolutions that have helped us move in the right direction and embrace our new life as Resolutionists. Come with us as we explain each resolution and how embracing it can improve your life. In the end, you too will be an energetic, fulfilled Resolutionist.

CHAPTER 1

THE TSUNAMI OF OUR LIVES

Never doubt that a small group of thoughtful, committed citizens can change the world. Indeed, it is the only thing that ever has.
—Margaret Mead

WHEN WE STARTED our corporate lives nearly forty years ago, expectations were very different. We would walk into the building dressed in the required conservative business attire— Patti in a below-knee-length skirt or  dress with a complementary blazer, Milledge in a dark suit, button-down white shirt, and conservative tie. We would stop by the clerical pool to pick up the stack of pink memo sheets, each with a different phone message. Then on to the typing pool to pick up any correspondence or reports we had dictated the day before, or maybe two days before. The office was noisy with the clicking of typewriter keys and high heels, as well as the ringing of phones and whir of copy and fax machines. It felt busy and exhilarating.

How little we knew about busy and exhilarating. Over the years, computers replaced typewriters, and email replaced snail mail. We videoconferenced with colleagues and clients all over the world and stored data in the cloud rather than a file drawer.

With the advances in technology over the decades, we would be the first to confirm Einstein's theory that time is relative. While the standard workday is still technically eight hours long, we fit so much more into it. If you asked for information, you often received it within hours rather than days. In fact, because so much was hosted on cloud-based servers, it was likely you could access your own data and not have to wait at all. Having the information sooner, however, meant you had to use that information sooner. Decisions that used to take weeks or months were now expected in days, hours, or sometimes minutes.

Technology allowed many workers to do their jobs from anywhere, anytime. And just like the *ability* to make decisions faster morphed into the expectation that decisions *would* be made faster, the ability to work anywhere, anytime morphed into the expectation that you would work 24-7.

This technology-based work process greatly increased productivity, which grew exponentially in the business sector, as more work was done by fewer people in less time. Beginning in 1973 the rate of productivity increased each decade until 2007, when the great financial crisis knocked everyone off their feet.[5] Now, with the addition of artificial intelligence systems, we are seeing another uptick in how much work can be produced in a day.

---

5   US Bureau of Labor Statistics as of February 6, 2020; https://www.bls.gov/lpc/prodybar.htm.

PATTI

On the first day of my first office job, I confidently entered the building dressed like all the other women. We all wore dresses or skirts that hit just below the knee, along with the required nude hose (no patterns or colors allowed). Pants, open-toed shoes, and colored nails were also forbidden. One time, when my flight was late, I showed up for a meeting with one of our most senior executives in a pair of pants—not jeans, a pair of dress slacks. After the meeting, I went back to my office to work, and he had his assistant call to remind me that pants were not appropriate. It was a monumental shift when the dress code was updated to allow women to wear slacks. Eventually, we had casual Fridays, where we could wear business casual attire. By the time I left, people—often including myself— were wearing jeans, T-shirts, and sometimes even flip- flops to work. As I was leaving my last full-time job and going out the door carrying my box of personal belongings, I was surrounded by intelligent, capable women and men working together in their designer blue jeans and vintage tees and enjoying a cappuccino. It felt like I had entered the corporate world thirty-five years earlier through a door that took me into a con- ventional environment, and now I was exiting through a door in the back of a Starbucks.

The relaxation of dress codes was one of many changes I experienced over my career. When I came into the business world, there was a very defined and respected hierarchy. When you got a promotion to the corner office, it was literally a corner office. Each rung up the ladder included increased responsibility and compensation, as well as an entire perk package. You might get a corporate car or an office with a bathroom, or you could choose three pieces of art from the corporation's inventory of art. I remember the last day I used the typing pool because I'd been promoted to the level that came with a personal secretary. By the time I left, it was very much an egalitarian environment, where CEOs often worked in conference room settings and personal secretaries were seen as elitist as opposed to productivity boosters. People still want to move up, but they no longer want to be surrounded by ostentatious trappings of power. Maybe the biggest change was that women *could* move up. Until 1978 women could legally be fired for being pregnant—and they were. Many companies didn't even hire married women. Back in the seventies, if you saw a woman walking down the hall, you assumed she was in a clerical position of some kind. The change from then to now, where women like me run our own companies and sit on boards—even in male-dominated industries—has been mind-blowing.

Career milestones also accelerated. When we started our careers, anyone promoted in five or six years was considered a superstar. By the time we retired, employees were getting nervous if they weren't promoted in six months. Some of today's tech companies have adjusted to this expectation by using six-month performance reviews rather than annual reviews to allow them to promote staff in small, incremental steps and play into their quick-progression expectations.

We saw the women's movement take off in the 1970s, when legislation opened up career and educational advancement. Although aimed at providing equal opportunity for women, the change in culture had profound consequences for men as well.

As women moved up the corporate ladder, they became equal financial partners at home. Men no longer were expected to be the sole or main breadwinner.

MILLEDGE

Looking at the changes that have occurred since my first day of work, I am most struck by how advances in technology and a change in culture—from having others do much of the work to "I'll do it myself"— has exponentially increased productivity. For example, if I wanted to put together a presentation at the beginning of my career, I would go to the company's library, research materials such as annual reports and economic data, and handwrite the report. I'd then take my yellow notepad pages to the typing pool and often wait several days to get a typed version back. If I or anyone else had changes, it had to go back to the pool for revisions. Then it had to go back through all the approvers to make sure everyone was OK with all of the edits. This usually took multiple iterations. Once finalized, the report was sent to the binding department to be bound; then I would personally get on an airplane to deliver it. Then we would wait for the client's reactions and start the process over again if he (it was always a he) had concerns.

Today, anyone in the office—not just certain people with access to the library—can put together presentations. While sitting at your own desk, you can access templates, graphics, and relevant data on the shared server. Everyone involved can edit the document directly and approve or reject edits almost instantaneously. You don't need to worry anymore that someone in the typing pool is unable to read your writing, makes a mistake in the transcription, and the report is delayed for days while the mistake is corrected. Instead of binding the presentation and delivering a hard copy, we can present it via videoconferencing to people around the world, all working through the deck at the same time. Concerns and questions can be handled in real time by the company's team of experts.

The speed of change, the speed of response, the connectivity and collaboration have all worked hand in hand to increase efficiency. And when you increase efficiency, you increase the ability of workers to do higher-level, more satisfying work.

The two-income family, with both partners having real careers, changed how we viewed our responsibilities to the family. Having two different careers going on meant that each partner was freer to take risks they might not have if they were the family's sole support.

We saw this play out in our own lives, as each of us has been able to grab riskier opportunities than we would have if we had not had the financial support of the other.

The ability to take on more risk has resulted in being more comfortable with risk. Thus one of the results of living through a tsunami of changes is this generation's ability to thrive with higher levels of risk, both professionally and personally. The rate of change in our generation was put on a new trajectory because people embraced risk and the changes it brought.

This risk tolerance has played out in lots of different ways. One of the not-so-obvious outcomes, but one that has a huge impact on this generation, is wealth creation. The boomer generation is the wealthiest generation in history. More people than ever have been able to shift socioeconomic classes because they were willing to take risks. This group has been able to aim high and take on risks that intimidated their parents because they aren't afraid of failure. What's the worst that can happen? You end up back where you started. What's the best that can happen? You reach your goals and move up to the next rung of the ambition ladder.

TIME TO TAKE THE NEXT STEPS

When we look at the traits that define the Resolutionist generation, it is easy to predict that "retirement" is going to be more than checking out the newest restaurant or visiting family. Our parents' generation grew up in the first half of the twentieth century and found comfort in rules, predictability, and knowing what was expected of them. "Duty before pleasure" could have been their motto. Our generation is certainly still responsible, but we aren't just working to provide for our families; we are more often motivated by the job itself—by the mental stimulation and sense of worth it provides, as well as the perks and prestige. While our parents' generation was rightly proud of negotiating a forty-hour work week during a time when workers were being exploited in factories, we embraced the fifty- and sixty-hour work week as a sign of success in the corporate world. No one referred to "workaholics" until our generation came on the scene.

PATTI

Timing is everything. The generation of women before me did not have the critical mass to change the culture. By the time I came along, I was able to be a part of a movement that found strength in numbers as opposed to trying to do it alone. There were other women who were balancing work and life and trying to get to the corner office, and so I didn't feel as alone as I might have in the generation before me. So being able to ride the women's movement, coupled with the expanded opportunities in the technology space, allowed me to make my way to places I never imagined I would go.

You are part of a confident, self-reliant group of people that grew up in an era of reform and believe they can change the world—in fact, they did. As noted earlier, they questioned established authority systems and challenged the status quo. Business models moved from hierarchal silos to collaborative teams. Regulations were passed to protect women and minorities in the labor force. Men and women took on equal responsibilities at home and in the office, with the role of breadwinner often being split within a couple. They embraced

x

the evolution of technology from typewriters to laptops, from rotary phones to videoconferencing, from magazines to social media. The advent of inexpensive Internet-based communications systems encouraged globalization and not only the ability but also the need to understand other cultures.

MILLEDGE

About five years into our marriage, Patti was CEO of a growing technology company. Her success in that role gave me the freedom to accept the opportunity to start an investment bank. A start-up technology bank was a risky proposition with as much chance of failing as succeeding. But I was able to take the risk on a start-up because Patti's situation was so stable. Then later, after Patti sold that company, she had an opportunity to take a position in Las Vegas. By that time the investment bank was doing well, and technology allowed managing the team and servicing clients from anywhere in the world. It was Patti's turn to take the risk with me being the one providing a stable income. We decided to take a chance and move to Las Vegas for Patti's career. Our great partnership allowed each of us to grab opportunities and advance our careers without risking our financial stability or our relationship.

We were recently visiting Stonehenge. While walking through the ruins, we were FaceTiming with our nieces, who were able to see in real time what we were seeing. We were able to have a discussion, ask and answer questions, and just generally bring two young girls in the United States along on our visit to England. This was a far cry from our day, when if we wanted to know about Stonehenge, we had to go to the library and rifle through the card catalog to find books and magazines—and then hope they were on the shelves—or skim through spools of black-and-white microfiche.

We have truly seen a tsunami of positive change in our lives.

We have truly seen a tsunami of positive change in our lives.

The societal and cultural shifts in the past four decades may not have been unprecedented—the advances in the fifteen years before and after 1900 were pretty tremendous—but they certainly were life changing for the people who lived through them.

It's no surprise that this group, with a life full of changes, would find it hard to settle into a traditional retirement. The difference between today's retirees and those of previous generations is that today's want and need to find meaning in their postcareer years, just as they did during their career. They want and need to be part of a like-minded community. This is not your parents' retirement.

WELCOME TO THE ANTI-RETIREMENT MOVEMENT

As we reached the time when we were ready to step away from hard-driving, time-consuming careers, we realized that we weren't ready to "retire." At least we weren't ready to stop being productive and adventurous. We had always initiated change and saw no reason we couldn't continue changing after our careers were over. If we were going to "retire," it was going to be on our own terms, or we weren't going to do it at all.

In the end we did leave our careers, but we would never call ourselves retired. We are busier now than we've ever been. The difference is that we are busy doing what brings us joy rather than what advances our careers.

We have entered a stage of life where we have the time and energy to explore, pursue a variety of endeavors that interest us, and use our time and knowledge to improve our personal, professional, and financial lives, as well as give back to our community. As we've talked to our friends and former work colleagues, we are finding that we are not alone. We are seeing people doing angel investments, starting companies, investing, lecturing at universities, mentoring, taking classes, and so much more. Our Resolutionist cohort is still doing a lot of work and still inspired—but we are doing it for ourselves and our community. This is "retirement" with a purpose. We are changing the paradigm of retirement the same way we changed the paradigm of work.

However, as we have found in our personal lives, you can't just attend the retirement party on Friday night and wake up Monday morning ready to embrace the next phase of your life. You need to prepare for going from a full, all-encompassing work life to a new reality that satisfies you but in different ways. Here in this phase, you can broaden your impact, work on your well-being—maybe for the first time ever—and expand your network of fellow norm-busters.

Believe us. We've been there. Transitioning from a results-oriented life with defined responsibilities and easily understood markers of success to an unstructured life that could stretch for the next thirty years isn't easy. We are still results-driven. We still look for measurements of success. But the metrics are different. They are not imposed from above. They are determined from within.

After experiencing what happens when you don't have a plan to ease that transition, we decided to write this book to help our fellow Resolutionist travelers avoid some of the potholes we tripped over. This book will introduce the areas of life most impacted when we leave the structure of full-time work and some suggested resolutions that can help make that impact positive versus negative. Not everyone will want or need to embrace every resolution, but taken as a whole, we believe these resolutions provide a workable framework for today's and tomorrow's Resolutionist.

As Fred Rogers (a.k.a. Mr. Rogers) so sagely noted, "Often when you think you're at the end of something, you're at the beginning of something else."

Onward to that "something else"!

CHAPTER 2

DEAR YOUNGER SELF

*Twenty years from now you will be more disappointed by the things that
you didn't do than by the ones you did do ... Explore. Dream. Discover.*

—Mark Twain

BACK IN THE late 1980s, we had a friend who decided to buy into
a franchise opportunity because he was frustrated with his corporate
job. He was a risk-taker, and staying with a large, rule-bound corporation was beginning to feel like a bad fit. He envisioned more autonomy,
more flexibility, more time at home, and more income. What he didn't
take into consideration was that the franchise service was completely
out of his wheelhouse. He had no experience in the product. He didn't
know the market. And, most importantly, he didn't have the financial
backing to see him through the lean start-up times while he got the
business going. He was a very good businessman, and he probably
could have overcome the negatives and made a success of the career
move—but the rising interest rates of the late eighties and the 1990
recession were enough to crumble his fledgling, underfunded enterprise. Thirty years later he is successful and happy with where he is in
life, but he still looks at that time as the one real mistake he made. It
put his family in financial jeopardy and limited what future risks they
could take. He still often wonders what his career would have been

like if he hadn't been so impetuous and stayed the corporate course.

It's easy to look back and know, with 20/20 hindsight, where you could have made different decisions in life. Some are just cringeworthy. Eighties hairstyle. The Macarena. Telling the boss that his business model was all wrong and you, a newly hired intern, would set him right.

You may also see other factors that impacted your career. Maybe you became a lawyer because your father was a lawyer, but looking back, you realize that wasn't really a good fit and you would have been happier in another profession. Maybe you stayed too long at a company with no advancement possibility. Or maybe you impulsively went the entrepreneurial route without the necessary skill set or financial backing. On the flip side, maybe talking to that stranger at the bus stop was the start of a marriage that lasted decades. Or maybe dropping out of the job market for two years to get your MBA proved to be the best decision you ever made.

We all make decisions based on the information we have at the time. Mostly, they work out. Sometimes they don't. And sometimes, even though you are generally satisfied with where you are in life, there are some things you would have changed if you had known then what you know now. When looking back at those decisions that worked well, you will likely see a pattern. And that pattern is planning. We have found that almost without exception, the more time and effort we put into planning, the better the outcome.

PLANNING WHEN THE FUTURE IS UNKNOWN

Planning for the future isn't easy. There is an entire industry of very well-paid futurists who travel the world speaking about what is to come. They are paid so well because accurately predicting the future isn't easy. Yet we are all asked to be futurists when it comes to planning for the time when we leave our full-time career.

Planning for the future, by definition, means we are looking beyond the horizon. The trick is to know how far to look. Very few twenty-five-year-olds are planning their postcareer lives before they have even started their now-career lives. That horizon is just too far away. Instead, we have rolling five- or ten-year plans as we move through our career, with the "retirement" horizon getting incrementally closer.

MILLEDGE

It took me a while to realize that it was time to leave full-time work. We were living in London, and Patti had officially entered her postcareer phase. However, I was still consulting for the bank that had acquired my previous company. In my mind, I wasn't stepping back—I was looking for my next full-time opportunity. Just before we were ready to leave on a three-week trip to Africa, I was approached by a prestigious bank to build their technology banking practice. It was an exciting role, and I told them I'd get back to them when I got back from Africa. But that trip to Africa changed everything. I realized I didn't want to be tied to a corporate life anymore. I wanted time to travel, learn, and give back on my own terms. I knew it was time for me to embrace the next phase in my life. That was my catalyst, my "ah-ha" moment.

Someplace around midcareer we begin asking ourselves how we will know it is time to leave. What are the catalysts or the signs in the tea leaves that will let you know you are ready for a change? Will you be ready to leave when you have accumulated a certain amount of wealth? Is it a certain amount of accomplishment? Will you work until your health gives out? Will you quit once your children are out of the house and on their own? Will you quit when your spouse does? There are a number of typical catalysts that encourage people to leave their full-time careers behind, but which ones apply to you are unique to your situation.

Knowing your catalysts can mean the difference between successfully transitioning to a fulfilled life after your career and boomeranging back to the full-time workforce simply because you didn't know why you quit to begin with.

> **Planning for the future, by definition, means we are looking beyond the horizon. The trick is to know how far to look.**

Despite our best of plans, however, life will always throw curveballs. Sometimes we have one catalyst in mind—perhaps a certain amount of financial security—and another one knocks us off our feet. It might be that you have an unexpected health scare, or maybe a parent is ill or dies young. Maybe you want to help your child with the grandchildren. Maybe a child or grandchild is an athlete or actor, and you want to enjoy their talent. Maybe you have been volunteering at a local charity, and you realize this is where you want to spend your time. Suddenly you are saying, "I didn't know this was a catalyst for me, but it is, and now I'm wondering how long I want to stay on this work treadmill versus moving to the next phase." So you have to have your plan, but you have to also be prepared to listen to the wake-up calls when they come, and they will come for everyone.

We know a woman, Lori, who was head of communications for the same company for thirty years. She loved the work and thought she would probably continue as long as she was able to contribute during strategy meetings, put out a coherent press release, and assemble an award-winning annual report. But, one day, she looked around and realized the management group she had worked with for decades was slowly changing as they reached retirement age. The CEO, the CFO, the chief investment officer—all were leaving in the next year or two. In fact, the company was actively looking to be acquired. It dawned on her that she liked her job but she liked it mainly because she liked the people she had worked with for so long. It would soon be a completely different company with different leaders and a different culture. It would not be the same job. And so she decided it was time to jump into the next phase of her life. Finding herself the last person of the original team still working wasn't a catalyst she had envisioned, but it turned out to be the one that created a clear signal that it was time to leave.

PATTI

I wish I had known earlier that I could redefine retirement to fit me. I wish I had known that I could be retired and still wear my skinny jeans and stiletto heels. I wish that I had known that my wisdom and experience would be valued. I wish I had known that I could say "goodbye" to the corporate world and still be interesting and relevant. I wish I had known that retirement is yours to define. I had successfully defined my role in the business world. I had joined the movement to organize sports for women, and I had balanced my life as a corporate leader and a mom. It didn't dawn on me that I could also reinvent retirement. I don't know why—it seems perfectly obvious now—I was convinced that I could redefine everything else in the world but not retirement.

Having a clear signal that it is time, however, doesn't always mean that you are truly prepared to leave the office behind, and Lori had some trouble transitioning simply because she had never pictured herself without full-time work. To make it all work, it helps to think through what is going to get you out of bed every morning. What are you going to do? What are you going to care about? Well before you are ready to cut the cake at your going away party, you want to plant the seeds for your Resolutionist life. Whether it's joining a corporate board, working with a nonprofit, volunteering, traveling, or whatever it may be, begin to build those passions so there is a seamless transition.

FIVE THINGS WE WISH WE'D KNOWN EARLIER

We have spent most of our life focused on building a successful career. What we were going to do when that career ended never entered our minds. No matter how old we were, it felt like we were still a long way away from walking away. But we are out of the full-time workforce now, and there a few things we wish we had known earlier. It would have made the transition so much easier!

ONE: RETIREMENT AIN'T WHAT IT USED TO BE.

We wish we had known, understood, and appreciated that earlier. We all have a vision of "retirement" built on what we've seen around us. We've watched our parents or grandparents settle into a quiet, nondescript life. We've seen the stereotypical portrayal of aging and irrelevant "retirees" on TV and in the movies. No one questions it. But we need to. We are not our fathers and mothers. This vision is not us.

TWO: WE HAVE MUCH MORE TIME IN THIS PHASE OF LIFE THAN PREVIOUS GENERATIONS.

This was a fact that hit us like an anvil when we read the Stanford longevity study. "Oh my God, this is a *thirty-year* phase." Some people will spend more years in their postcareer life than they did building their career. We hadn't fully appreciated that. Knowing and understanding what that means will help you plan better.

PATTI

Because we have so much time left on this earth, I wish I had known that managing your health is important from the beginning to the end. It's not something you start managing when you turn fifty or sixty. I wasn't very good at managing my health. I burned the candle at both ends. I worked crazy hours. I didn't get the physical exercise I should have. I ate all the wrong foods at the endless business dinners. I think if I had realized how much more important your health becomes as you age, I would have done things differently. It seems common sense, but I don't think you really think about long-term health when you're younger and you're trying to get everything done. I wish I had known that I was going to have such a long retirement. I would have thought differently about managing my health earlier, to get the benefits at this stage of my life.

THREE: ALWAYS BE PLANNING FOR THE NEXT PHASE.

We should have been planning for our Resolutionist life earlier than we did. The horizon is closer than it looks.

FOUR: YOU NEED TO REDEFINE YOUR METRICS.

We wish we had known that we needed to redefine how we measure success in this phase because it's different from our previous metrics. If we had thought that through earlier, it would have been an easier transition. Instead, the goals are likely to be more qualitative than quantitative. For example, one of our metrics one year was to enhance our celebrations. We found that many holidays and special events were filled with unnecessary stress and were too materially focused. We decided to eliminate event-driven gift giving from our relationship as a method of changing this dynamic. If we wanted something special, we would seek it out together—avoiding the cadence that is set by the holiday calendar. We didn't know how much our lives would improve by making this simple change. Our goal of more festivity and less stress was accomplished. Now our special days are focused on why they are special and *not* what we are gifting one another.

FIVE: BEING A RESOLUTIONIST IS FUN.

If someone had told us when we were in our thirties that our "retirement" years would be so much more filled with fun, laughter, and fulfillment, we would have never believed it in a million years. We laugh more now than we've laughed at any other stage in our life. This phase is instilled with so much adventure, and it's a feeling that comes from within rather than the happiness of achieving a certain stock price.

IT'S NEVER TOO EARLY—OR TOO LATE—TO START PREPARING

We have also learned, and wished we knew earlier, that preparing for these years is a process and what you need to do for the future depends on where you are today. If you are early in your career, you have decades to plan and prepare. The closer you get to leaving the workforce the more focused your preparation needs to be. However, it's never too late to make your Resolutionist years more fulfilling and satisfying. Just look at where you are, where you want to be, and get going.

IF YOU ARE YEARS FROM LEAVING THE FULL-TIME WORKFORCE

Congrats! You have time to get mentally prepared. That's the good news—it's also the bad news. The problem with having lots of time is that it is human nature to put off whatever can be put off. When there never seem to be enough hours in the day to get everything done that must be done, it's easy to push off thinking about retirement until you suddenly look up and realize, "It's here!" But you will find the transition easier if you find some time to think about what you want to do in these less-hectic years. Well before you are looking at life after career, begin thinking about what brings you joy. What are your passions? Are there opportunities, hobbies, or volunteer activities you wish you had more time for? Are there adventures you'd like to have?

PATTI

I wish I had known that this phase of life is so much more dimensional than at any other phase because you are in the sandwich. You're typically dealing with aging parents, as well as adult children. You're multitasking more than ever. You're dealing with things that are more nuanced, as your parents age and as you age and as your children become adults. You're not just managing activity; you have to add thought and creativity to it. I thought that when I got to retirement, my plate would be clean. I wouldn't have to do anything. And then you get here, and you realize that's not really the case. Maybe you have grandchildren. Maybe you're managing three or four generations. Maybe you're dealing with not just your own financial situation but the financial situation of your parents or siblings. Maybe not just your health but the health of your parents and maybe even the health of your friends and loved ones. I think there are so many more dimensions here than you think there are going to be when you're just trying to get that next promotion and raise your kids and buy that house. It seems like you go from transactional life to more of a nuanced impact on people's lives at this stage. I feel so much more emotionally invested than earlier in my life. I wish I had known that. I probably would have prepared myself differently than I did.

With several years until retirement, you can begin preparing for what you want to do. For example, after he left his corporate job, Bill was able to seamlessly transition to his true passion of being a college professor because he had spent decades planning and preparing for the career change. During the years while he was moving around the country and up the ranks in his marketing career, he often took on adjunct assignments at nearby universities, teaching at night and on weekends. The pay was negligible, and he certainly didn't need to fill more hours in his week, but he loved teaching, and the experience was invaluable. By the time he was ready to leave his primary career, he had years of teaching experience on his resume, in addition to being considered an expert in his field. He had no trouble finding the right university for his skills.

Another thing to begin thinking about during this time is: What gives you a sense of purpose? Our jobs and families often give us a sense of purpose during our working years. But what are you going to replace that with when the kids move out, you've acquired financial security, you've achieved your career goals, and it's time to stop working? We need a reason to get out of bed in the morning. Many successful people use their Resolutionist years to give back in some way. They might serve on the board of a favorite charity, work with a foundation to support its mission, get involved in local politics, or mentor younger people coming up through their former industry. However, it often surprises people how adrift they feel without the structure of full-time work. They thought they would be happy just relaxing and pursuing hobbies they hadn't had time for before. What they didn't realize is that we all need to be needed. Begin to narrow down the things that provide fulfillment before you jump in and the transition to "retirement" will be much easier.

As much as possible, this is the time to determine what your catalysts will be as you come toward the time to step into your post-career phase. We talked about the importance of catalysts earlier, so what will indicate to you that it's time to move to the next phase? These often involve reaching a financial milestone or the final rung on the corporate ladder, or maybe it's reaching the end of a long-term project. Whatever it is, you want to have a goal so you don't just find yourself drifting into an after-career life rather than controlling the narrative.

Finally, when you are doing all of this planning and dreaming about the future, it is important to include others that your decision will affect. It's rare that two people are in the exact same place at the exact same time. As you're looking at the next phase, make sure you're talking to those around you who will have some input and sway in the decision.

IF YOU ARE IN THE MIDST OF LEAVING
THE FULL-TIME WORKFORCE

If you are staring "retirement" in the face but didn't prepare for it in your younger years, you might want to ease into this new phase gradually. Maybe you could continue to work for another two years so that you have time to take some of the steps outlined above. Or maybe you could continue to work, but in a different occupation, such as consulting or writing, until you've done some of the above steps to help prepare you for what can be a confusing time. Or maybe you really do just want to step away and decompress for six months or a year before you decide how you are going to structure the rest of your life. If that is the case, go for it. But at the same time, lay the groundwork for the years that follow. Nearly everyone is happier when they are engaged in activities that fulfill them.

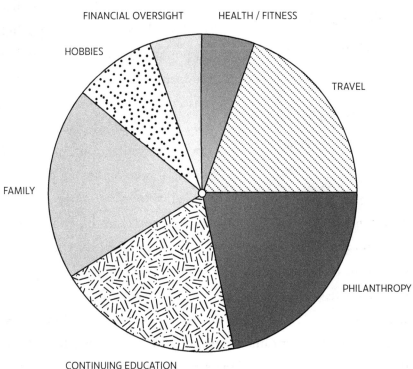

TIME SPENT DURING POSTCAREER

To make sure life doesn't just drift forever, it helps to have a real plan. We're not talking about a twenty-page bound document. A single Excel sheet or whiteboard scribble will do. But knowing where you want to spend your time will make transitioning to your after-career life so much easier. Building a plan for your Resolutionist life is similar to building a portfolio of investments. You start with what you want the portfolio to do. Maybe you have designed your investment portfolio so that when you reach sixty-five, it will be generating a specific amount of income for the next thirty years. To achieve that goal, you have been very purposeful in populating the portfolio with a diversified mix of investments. Each has a role in providing the outcome you need. Making a plan for retirement is similar, but instead of financial assets filling your portfolio, you are creating a portfolio that is filled with ways to use your time. Sit down and do a little pie chart. How much time do you want to spend on your health? How much with your family? Do you want to spend time investing your money? Do you want to spend time giving back? Do you want to spend it on hobbies—golf, running, painting, and so on? Do you want to travel, take continuing education classes, continue to work part-time? Everyone's portfolio will be different, but the end result will likely be the same—a life filled with a sense of purpose and fulfillment.

Building a plan for your Resolutionist life is similar to building a portfolio of investments.

While we firmly believe everyone needs a plan as they leave their full-time career, we also know that retirement is a process and things will change over time. The first couple of years of our "retirement" looked very different than our life now. And that's OK. No one knows how entering the Resolutionist phase will affect them until they are actually in the middle of it. We have found that it helps to have shorter-term goals that will give you a sense of success until you have settled into your personal "retirement" model and the future is clearer.

This planning doesn't stop once you step away from your career. In fact, it might be even more important because you discover that all that time you thought you had to accomplish your goals is actually limited by finances, health, other commitments, or simply the number of hours in a day. So how do you get it all done? You plan! Then you execute. The plan is useless if there is no follow-through.

We are currently putting together a five-year plan to figure out what we want to be doing during that time frame and to envision what we want to look like five years from now. For us, planning for the future never stops.

IF YOU ARE ALREADY IN THE POSTCAREER PHASE

Have you already left the full-time workforce but feel unsatisfied with the traditional retirement? That might be because your vision of these years, which was probably formed when you were in your twenties or thirties, doesn't match with reality. Too often we view postcareer as simply time to relax and indulge in hobbies such as golf or fishing. But life is multidimensional. Your work was multidimensional. "Retirement" needs to be too.

So if you're miserable, take a step back and ask, "How do I add other dimensions to my life?"

You do it by deploying all the tools that we are suggesting in this book, which focus on finding new metrics, a new community, and a new purpose for this stage of life. The early phases of "retirement" are the prime time to put our twelve resolutions into practice, become a Resolutionist, and ease your way back into a more active lifestyle.

THE NUMBER ONE THING WE WOULD TELL OUR YOUNGER SELVES

This is your choice. You get to choose how you live this stage of your life. You don't need to twist yourself into an outdated model. Simply changing how we look at "retirement" can make a huge difference. "Retirement" isn't the default state of choosing to leave work. It's the state you are choosing to enter.

PART II

THE RESOLUTIONS

THE YEARS AFTER you leave your full-time career can be the best years of your life for learning, leading, and giving. It is the phase of life when you still have high-level skills, an abundance of energy, wisdom gained from experience, and the time to put it all together for a purposeful life. But fully embracing your Resolutionist years requires a different mindset than the one that served you so well during your career. The structure and metrics that succeeded in your corporate life will probably not work in your postcareer life. That doesn't mean you don't need structure and metrics to measure success. You absolutely do. But you will need a different sort of structure and metrics because what defines success will be different.

Through trial and error, we have found twelve tools (i.e., resolutions) that have helped us build a "retirement" that lets us continue to learn, grow, and contribute, as opposed to slowly drifting away. The resolutions focus on actions to help you change your mental outlook from one defined by career and corporate goals to one defined by personal and community goals. They will change you from a corporate warrior to a Resolutionist in the anti-retirement movement, as you learn to look at the world in a completely different way. You might not need or want to use each one. That's fine. That's the beauty of the anti-retirement movement. It is not one-size-fits-all. It's do what fits you. But if you are struggling to leave work behind, we hope our resolutions will help make it easier. They certainly made it easier for us!

RIP THE BAND-AID OFF

There are no gains without pains.

—Benjamin Franklin

AS DENNIS WAS FINISHING his fourth decade as a successful corporate lawyer, he realized that his work activities were no longer fulfilling. He thought about retiring then and there, but the chairman of the firm told him, "You need a plan. And golf is not a

plan." Dennis realized he didn't have a plan—and he didn't play golf. So he worked for another two years while he formulated a plan to leave. He really thought he was ready on that last day in December. But then, the next week, he remembered that he had left his Keurig coffee maker in the office and needed to retrieve it. While there, he thought he really needed to clean out his desk, organize the books, decide what to throw away and what to keep. He spent the next few months going into the office every day, going through everything he had accumulated in the past forty years and sitting in on the occasional meeting. He just couldn't let go. Then his wife planned a three-week trip to Yosemite. She was ready to begin the next phase of their life, even if Dennis wasn't. Dennis had gotten involved in environmental issues a couple of years before, and this was a dream trip. It opened his eyes to what he really wanted to do with his time—and it wasn't taking old law books to the recycling center.

MILLEDGE

Patti and I have been practicing Band-Aid ripping from the beginning. When we decided to get married, I was living and working in Dallas, while Patti's job was in Kansas City. We decided that when we married, we would make a clean break. I would sell my companies. She would quit her job. And we would start fresh in the California Bay Area and build a new life together. That was truly a Band-Aid-ripping experience!

The trip also helped him change his habit of going into the office each day. He was finally able to put his career behind him and embrace his new life.

Dennis isn't alone in his separation anxiety experience when it came to leaving his full-time job. In fact, a recent survey from RAND Corporation found almost 40 percent of workers over sixty-five had previously, at some point, retired.[6]

So failing at retirement would seem to be relatively common. For a lot of people, moving from the excitement and fulfillment of a career to the quietness of retirement is too much. They end up retreating to the environment that has provided their self-worth for much of

---

6   Nicole Maestas, Kathleen J. Mullen, David Powell, Till von Wachter, Jeffrey B. Wenger, *Working Conditions in the United States* (Santa Monica, CA: RAND Corporation, 2019), 2.

their life. Sometimes that is going back to their original job, but more often it is doing something similar that seems more interesting than retirement at the time.

For example, Lori, the communications executive we mentioned earlier, found herself being pulled back into a full-time job soon after retiring. The CEO she had worked with for years was starting an environmental foundation to encourage sustainable practices in their industry and wanted her help. She jumped at the opportunity, thinking it was going to recreate the work atmosphere she missed. How wrong she was. It turned out that the CEO was great at running an established corporation but not so great at building an enterprise from the ground up. It was an unpleasant experience, and she was happy to leave when the group was absorbed into a larger trade organization. She thought that she was really heading to retirement this time, but she still wasn't mentally in the right place. When a European environmental group reached out and offered her a four-month contract, complete with several trips to the European headquarters, she grabbed it. By the time her contract was over, she had helped the group establish itself as a player in the industry, and she was ready to leave. This time, she was really ready. She was going out on top, and it was time to move on.

PATTI

I did everything wrong when it came to my first retirement (yes, you read that right—I've "retired" more than once). I didn't have a specific catalyst. It just seemed time. More importantly, I didn't have a plan. I simply walked out of my office one day and into "retirement" the next, without any idea of what I would do with my time. It's no surprise then that after a couple of years flitting from one activity to another, I ended up back in the workforce. This time, however, I planned for my postcareer life so that it would actually stick. I knew what catalysts would let me know it was time, and I made sure I had things that would give my life a sense of purpose. The first day of my second "retirement," I woke up and said, "From now on, I'm not going to apologize for being retired. I'm going to see it as an accomplishment, like so many other things in my life have been. This is not an end; it is a beginning." The second time around has been nothing like a traditional retirement—it's an anti-retirement, and I've never been happier. Planning and preparing—and reframing how I viewed my new world—made all the difference.

Sometimes one person is ready to leave the full-time workforce and their partner agrees to leave at the same time but they really aren't ready. We have friends, Barry and Janine, who stepped back from their careers several years ago. They wanted to make a clean break—rip the Band-Aid off, so to speak—so they bought an old farmhouse in Tuscany. For the next five years, they spent their time renovating the house and growing olives. Barry loved every minute of being the gentleman farmer "under the Tuscan sun." Janine was keeping busy learning Italian and overseeing the renovations. She loves languages, and it had always been a dream to one day be able to really immerse herself in a foreign language and culture. It was nice, but it wasn't bringing her happiness the way living in Tuscany was enjoyable to Barry.

About five years after making the move, Janine received a call asking if she would be interested in returning to work and helping a company that was reinventing itself. She hadn't realized how much she missed the challenge and day-to-day interactions of her corporate career until she received that phone call. She and Barry moved to London, where Barry could enjoy his continued retirement near family and Janine could manage the firm's European operations. Several years in the company was sold, and Janine realized that now, finally, she was ready to really step back. This time, she was making a proactive decision rather than following another's lead. Being mentally ready to "retire" has made all the difference.

THE NEXT PHASE IS AS MUCH A MENTAL STATE AS A PHYSICAL ONE

We could go on with several more examples of failed attempts at retirement, but they all share one common factor—the people leaving the workforce did so because they thought it was time to leave their jobs but they weren't mentally prepared. We tend to think about retirement as "the absence of full-time work." Physically, that's easy to see. You simply leave the office one day and stay home the next. But how do you mentally make that transition? How do you move from thinking about work 24-7 (yes, many of us feature work events in our dreams) to not thinking about it at all?

We have found that those who make the easiest transition to "retirement" are able to make a clean break from their past life. For Dennis, he needed to enter the magical world of Yosemite to get over his separation anxiety. For us, it involved a move to London for two years. For Barry, it was immersing himself in the Italian olive oil industry.

When it came time to move beyond our traditional careers, we knew that we needed to make a dramatic change from our working life. If we didn't completely disconnect from our work, we would continue to be pulled into meetings and consultations, and one day we would look around and realize we were back to work. Patti had already experienced this very common phenomenon. So for us, that dramatic break meant moving to London, where we remained for more than two years. When we returned to the United States, our previous careers no longer held any sway over us.

During this time we also built a new home that suited the next phase of our lives better. Living in London gave us the physical and mental distance we needed from our previous careers, but we wanted to make sure that we were able to keep that distance when we returned to the United States. We knew we couldn't return to the status quo, live in the same house we'd been living in for fifteen years, in the same neighborhood, and slip back into doing what we had always done—or we would probably not change our trajectory. We had to fully rip the Band-Aid off.

We know a fellow who did something similar. He was a serial CEO of start-up companies. When he did his last one, he and his wife got on a boat and traveled around the world for a year. That is advanced Band-Aid ripping.

Look to disrupt your life in ways that cause you to create new patterns, new behaviors, new circles of friends, and stimulate your brain in a different way.

Although this particular friend found sailing around the world the best way to break from work and his old life and we found moving to London and returning to a different house than we had left the best option for us, others have found less dramatic but just as effective ways to make that break. The key is to find activities and interests that fill your life so you don't miss the office. Look to disrupt your life in ways that cause you to create new patterns, new behaviors, new circles of friends, and stimulate your brain in a different way.

Science has found that habits—including going into work every day—have three main parts: a cue, a routine, and a reward.[7] If you can disrupt any of the three parts, you can change the habit. Thus Band-Aid ripping works so well because it removes the cues and routines that support the impulse to keep living your old life. However, to make it easier to give up your old life, you will want to replace it with something that provides the same type of reward you got from work, something that keeps you engaged, relevant, growing, and enthused. The possibilities are almost endless.

We know a woman who was CEO of a software company but decided in her fifties to rip the Band-Aid off by going to medical school. Surrounding yourself with bright twenty-somethings is certainly going to create new thought patterns. We have friends who have gone to culinary school. They don't just want to cook a better meatloaf. They want to be chef-quality cooks. Another friend left his law practice to take an intensive one-year university certificate program. He doesn't have time to be tempted by his old world anymore.

Some people take up a language. Some learn a musical instrument. Some research their family history, including traveling to places their ancestors once lived and meeting distant cousins. Some take on a physical challenge, such as running a marathon or a 10K race. Some focus on artistic pursuits and display their creations at local fairs. We've seen people take up wine making and buy a winery. We've seen

---

7   Cassie Shortsleeve, "5 Science-Approved Ways to Break a Bad Habit," *Time* online, August 28, 2018, https://time.com/5373528/break-bad-habit-science/.

people purchase a bed-and-breakfast in an area where they've always wanted to live.

A number of people choose philanthropy as their Band-Aid ripping. We've met people who tell us: "We're going to go to a philanthropy workshop to learn how to set up a foundation." "We're going to go on a retreat to learn how it is all done." "We're going to go with a number of different nonprofits on some of their mission trips to learn more about that." This is different than writing a check or volunteering at an annual event. You now have the time and energy to dive deep and find ways to satisfy your soul when it comes to making a difference.

The idea is to do something in a new way that totally engages you and replaces whatever "reward" you got from your full-time job so you are not wishing you were back in the career-driven world. The people we know who have made a clean break are in a happier state at this stage of life than people who didn't make that break.

We have a friend who thought this was just more days of golf. Instead of playing two days a week, he was looking forward to playing five days a week. But he got bored very quickly, and he went back to work. However, this particular job was also unfulfilling, and he ended up leaving it. Now, he's tackling "retirement" in a different way.

The problem he ran into during his first attempt was that he viewed retirement as one-dimensional. He was finally going to be able to play golf every day. But life isn't one-dimensional. Your career wasn't singularly focused. When you're working full-time, you're doing lots of things. You're managing people, you're managing customers, you're launching new products, and you're talking to investors—you're doing all these things. The more you do, the more energized you are.

So when people decide to be singularly focused—golf, fishing, sailing, reading—it wears pretty quickly. You are used to a multidimensional life and suddenly your life has gotten very small. That's what drives a lot of the dissatisfaction people have with retirement and sends them back to work.

In a conversation about this topic, a friend gave us sage advice. In his estimation, if you have a hobby that you enjoy during your career (golf, fishing, gardening, etc.), add 10 to 15 percent more of it in retirement instead of making it your full-time pursuit. This allows you time to find other interests and passions in this next phase of your life.

PREPARING TO RIP THE BAND-AID OFF

If you are going to rip the Band-Aid off, you need to prepare for it. Otherwise, you're likely to apply a fresh Band-Aid and nothing will have been accomplished.

A friend of ours is selling his business. If all goes well, the closing will occur very soon. He is already preparing for the next phase by making a list of things he might want to consider doing. Whenever something catches his eye, he adds it to the list. So far, he has a list of more than twenty things that he's going to prioritize as he researches each of them.

It's important to note that you aren't just ripping the Band-Aid off for the sake of doing it. Whatever activity or goal you engage in should be something you really want to do. We chose to relocate to London because we love travel, we thrive on experiencing different places, and we wanted to see more of the world. You might want to get involved in your local theater group, become an expert in the stock market, or find homes for retired greyhound dogs. The activity doesn't matter. What matters is that it frees you from your work life and enables you to move forward. It's really about shocking your system into changing your patterns and behavior.

MOVING FORWARD

Some people enter retirement believing that they won't be attracted to work again. They have left for a reason; why would they want to go back? The answer is that it is hard to develop new patterns. You've spent thirty or forty years immersed in the structure and culture of a career. Now you are expected to reinvent your life. It's hard! Suddenly, you don't really remember why you left.

You don't remember the endless trips on airplanes and the sleepless nights preparing for presentations. All you remember is winning that new account or getting that well-deserved promotion and how awesome it all was. People tend to miss the things that they liked, and they forget about the things that they were ready to leave behind. When life gets uncomfortable, we look to revert back to those things that gave us comfort in the past.

In our next chapter, we'll talk about embracing the uncomfortable. It's how you grow and continue to gain confidence. You'll learn to love being uncomfortable. That's true anti-retirement!

GIVE IT A TRY

- Identify the personal Band-Aid that is linking you to your professional life—examples could be attending industry events, stopping by your old office, following your previous company on social media, frequenting the same business lunch spots, and the like.

- Embrace disruptors to your past patterns. You might consider taking a short- or long-term residency in a new location, unsubscribing from trade newsletters, or immersing yourself in a new skill, language, or hobby.

GET COMFORTABLE WITH THE UNCOMFORTABLE

Life begins at the end of your comfort zone.

—Neale Donald Walsch

A FRIEND OF OURS ran his own company for thirty years. After all those years, he was very confident that he could solve any problem that arose. Going into work every day, growing his company, managing employees—all were in his comfort zone. Then he sold the company. Suddenly life was different. He and his wife fell into a peaceful routine. They gardened, watched TV, took long walks, cooked dinner, and went to bed together at the same time every night. It was a serene life, but after the excitement of building a successful enterprise, he needed more. He wanted to do something that got his blood flowing and his brain engaged again. After a few starts and stops, he took up long-distance cycling, which involved monthlong bicycle rides. Forcing himself to get away and try something different that involved meeting new people and experiencing the uncertainty of not knowing where he was going to stop each night was exactly what he needed. Being uncomfortable yet persevering made him feel alive. He was growing and learning each day. He didn't need his work to make him feel capable. He was finding new ways.

Our friend had unintentionally stumbled on one of the main drivers of happiness—stepping out of your comfort zone. It would seem counterintuitive to think that being uncomfortable brings happiness, but it does. Let's look at why.

When we are uncomfortable, our anxiety level rises. Instinctively, we want to reduce that anxiety. This is where the "fight or flight" instinct kicks in. Unless the situation is truly dangerous, the best course of action to take is typically "fight." This doesn't literally mean fighting—at least not most of the time. It means resolving the conflict or dissonance that is causing the anxiety. By embracing uncomfortable situations—taking on a big project, speaking at a conference, learning a new skill set—we develop the self-confidence that enables us to take on additional risks. The same psychological benefits of stepping outside your comfort zone can be found in the Resolutionist stage of your life.

PATTI

During my career, I spent years eating at a variety of restaurants all over the world. Yet I had never learned to use chopsticks. I found great comfort in request-ing utensils when dining at an Asian restaurant, even though everyone else was using chopsticks. So when I committed to embracing something new at the beginning of my postcareer phase, I decided it was time to learn to eat with chopsticks. The first time I ate an entire Asian meal without using a knife, fork, or spoon, I was on top of the world. Firsts always stay with you. It goes back to that first kiss you had. It goes back to that first A you got on your report card and that first medal that got hung around your neck. Who knew that you could still experience firsts at this stage of life?

When we "retire" and are no longer required to be part of uncomfortable work situations, we often simply avoid the discomfort, which leads to diminished levels of confidence. Instead of letting yourself get in a rut, go at life as if it's an adventure—because it is. You will be disappointed sometimes. But when you accomplish something you didn't think you could—mastering a new language, cycling across your state, or selling your painting at an art fair—you get a jolt of endorphins that drives you to your next challenge. There is no substitute for achieving something for the first time when it comes to building confidence.

At this stage of life, if you're not forcing yourself into the unknown often enough, your self-confidence starts to wane. If you want to continue living your best life and being interested and interesting, you have to continue pushing the boundaries.

A friend of ours who is in his midseventies decided that he was going to learn something new every single month. That's the kind of thing that will help him stay young, live longer, and be more interesting and engaged. Now that is a Resolutionist!

Feeling good about yourself stems from trying and accomplishing new things. The accomplishment doesn't have to be gigantic. It just has to be something you haven't done before. It reminds you how resilient you are, reminds you how capable you are. And it feels so good.

We have another friend who decided to write her memoir. She enrolled in a memoir-writing class and, by the end, had a novella-length story of her life. She was as proud of that memoir as she was of any of her career accomplishments. We need to be fed by those endorphins as we age, just like we were fed by them when we were younger.

If you are doing things that interest you, you will be more interesting to others, which is an important part of this stage. It doesn't have to be something grandiose. For example, we decided to learn a new dance. Neither of us had ever felt comfortable dancing, but it was something we wanted to try. So we took lessons, practiced, laughed at ourselves, and soon began to feel that dancing might be in our comfort zone after all. When we were ready, we filmed ourselves and sent video dance challenges to friends. It was a great way to stay in touch, and we plan to use our new dancing skills at every opportunity.

ESCAPE HATCH

How do you embrace the uncomfortable knowing that not everything will go according to plan? Will I enjoy a new cuisine, a fresh form of entertainment, or a physical challenge the first time? To reduce risk and encourage the exploration of new horizons, we instituted the concept of the "escape hatch." The concept allows any member of the party to terminate the activity at any time—no judgment, no guilt. We have found that its very existence allows us to try many more uncomfortable activities than we would have in ordinary circumstances. We are much more willing to take risks when it is measured and have used the "escape hatch" several times.

An example is that we planned to attend a black-tie event in our local community—good cause, good venue. We realized very quickly that it was grossly overcrowded, lacked organization, and would extend well past our bedtime. When the time was right, we "raised our paddle," made a donation, looked at each other, and pulled the "escape hatch." Soon, we were on our way home, dressed to the nines with a warm bag of fast food in hand.

We also extend the "hatch" to our guests. We treated one of our friends to a night at the London Theatre to take in an acclaimed performance. In the first act, we could all sense that this risk was not going to pay off. At intermission we locked eyes and said, "I need an escape." So off we went into a rainy London night—none the worse for wear.

But most times the safety net that comes with knowing that you have an escape creates a willingness to go to new places, sample unusual flavors from around the world, or learn something for the first time. Measured risk drives adventure—and if you need an escape, it is there.

MOVING FORWARD

When you approach stepping out of your comfort zone, don't think about it as one and done. The idea isn't to be uncomfortable for the sake of being uncomfortable. It's to develop new skills, learn new things, meet new people, and stretch your mind in ways that will all make your Resolutionist life more fun and fulfilling. It is only by overcoming our discomfort that we grow and continue to stumble on those things that bring joy.

GIVE IT A TRY

- Identify five activities that sit at the edge of your comfort zone—for example, sample an exotic cuisine, enjoy an unfamiliar art form, or embark on a unique adventure.

- At the right time and with the right amount of courage, take the leap.

- Discuss your experience with a friend or family member.

- Rinse and repeat!

PRIORITIZE YOURSELF

Your time is limited; don't waste it living someone else's life.

—Steve Jobs

MAKING YOURSELF A priority doesn't come naturally to most of us. We are so used to being of service to others—our bosses, employees, shareholders, clients, family, friends—that it seems selfish to spend time on ourselves. In fact, the last time many of us ever felt comfortable putting our own needs first was when we were young children.

But this stage of our lives is different. After decades of putting the needs of others first, it is now time to focus our energies on what we want to do. It's not only time, but it's also important that we do so. Why?

First of all, you've earned it. Putting yourself first means you don't really need a good reason to do so. The fact that you want to do something should be enough. But there really are very good objective reasons to prioritize yourself.

Mental and physical health and wellness are an important part of this stage. We all like to think we're as healthy as we have always been—and for some of us, that might actually be true. But for the majority of those entering a postcareer life, physical challenges begin to pop up more frequently than before. In addition, this is a time when some people begin to experience depression for the first time. Everything is changing, and they aren't sure what their purpose is any more. By giving yourself permission to focus on those things that bring you happiness, you will positively contribute to your outlook on life. And, according to the Mayo Clinic,[8] having a positive outlook on life may contribute to:

- Increased life span

- Lower rates of depression

- Lower levels of distress

- Greater resistance to the common cold

- Better psychological and physical well-being

- Better cardiovascular health and reduced risk of death from cardiovascular disease

- Better coping skills during hardships and times of stress

Who wouldn't want to jump onto that list of benefits, particularly when it simply involves prioritizing yourself? Well, there's no "simple" to it. Changing habits built over a lifetime isn't easy. But we have found a few ways to help.

PATTI

Whenever I would experience some sort of upheaval in my personal life, I would embrace the safety and comfort of work. I took on extra projects, traveled

---

8   Mayo Clinic Staff, "Positive thinking: Stop negative self-talk to reduce stress," January 21, 2020, https://www.mayoclinic.org/healthy-lifestyle/ stress-management/in-depth/positive-thinking/art-20043950.

more than was probably necessary, and just generally filled every minute of my time with work-related activities. Then, my younger brother died. It was a shock, and I dealt with it the way I always dealt with these sorts of things—I threw myself into my work. But this time, I wasn't finding the satisfaction I had in the past. My brother had dreams of what he wanted to do—traveling to the places he wanted to see, visiting relatives around the world, and prioritizing his own health. His death was the real catalyst that made me realize that my work was no longer a "safe place" but something that distracted me from what I really wanted to be doing. I understood that my grief, my emotions, and my family were my priority. The more I prioritized myself, the better the person I became.

IT REALLY IS ALL ABOUT YOU

During our career years, work itself took up most of the day. It wasn't unusual to miss family dinners or set aside hobbies because a work project needed to be completed or a meeting ran long.

Now all of that has changed. Your priority has been your work output. Now it is you. As hard as it is to leave the comfort of the corporate structure, ripping the

The mental jump you want to make is moving from "How will this help my career or my company?" to "How will this help me and bring me happiness?"

Band-Aid off and getting comfortable with the uncomfortable actually helps with this stage. Without your employer clamoring for your attention, you are free to focus elsewhere.

One of the hardest things to do at this stage is to reframe your priorities so that the things that you want to do are viewed as just as valid as any work priority ever was. We often view a day at the spa or learning to paint as frivolous. Yet why is mental and physical health viewed as frivolous?

Everyone needs to free themselves from the idea that some things are more worthy of their time than others. We aren't looking to focus on what is "worthy"; we are looking to focus on what makes us happy and healthy. The mental jump you want to make is moving from "How will this help my career or my company?" to "How will this help me and bring me happiness?"

HOW DO YOU PRIORITIZE YOURSELF?

To really prioritize yourself, you need to be purposeful. You are trying to develop a completely new way of thinking—a way that matches where you are in life now rather than where you used to be. That means you need to develop concrete strategies to keep from falling into your old patterns.

We have found that a virtual whiteboard where we collect ideas of things we want to do has worked for us. Your whiteboard can be virtual or actual. A piece of paper, phone app, sticky note, or anything else that works for you is fine. The goal is to capture ideas of things to do as you see, read, or hear about them. These ideas can range from trying a new restaurant to going skydiving, or from checking out a local winery to learning a new language. Some of the ideas involve things that we both want to do, while others are personal. We don't self-censor at this stage; we just jot down anything that interests us. In this way, we always have a list of possibilities that is constantly being renewed and is evergreen.

PATTI

Soon after I stepped back from my career, we were moving into our new next-stage house, and I was organizing my closet. As I put away my wardrobe, I realized, "I don't have anything to wear." Half of my closet was dictated by my business life, and the other half was dictated by my fitness regimen. So I basically had exercise clothes and business clothes. I had nothing else. For the first time, I didn't have to follow a dress code. I could wear whatever made me happy. That was both freeing and a huge burden. There weren't rules anymore. I didn't have to look a certain way. I didn't have to wear certain things. And that was, for me, one of my very first projects, where I said, "OK, this is all about me. This isn't about meeting someone else's expectations." And off on a shopping trip I went!

Once you have a list of possibilities, you are going to have to prioritize. One way to divide and prioritize is to look at the required time commitment. You might group local or personal activities that would only take a couple of hours to complete, while others that take planning or training would be in another group. Within these groups, you could prioritize by how much you really want to do them. For example, you might have wanted to run a marathon ever since you saw Robert Kiprono Cheruiyot win his fourth Boston Marathon in

2010. Now you have time to train and actually make that goal a reality, so you move that to the top. Goals that you want to do someday but don't feel driven to put the time into now can remain on the list but would be moved down. You might find that next year, a few of these items begin to take on more importance and move up the list. Or maybe they don't. And that's OK.

You do not want your whiteboard of possibilities to become a "must-do" list. Do not let yourself fall back into work mode, where you completed goals because you had to. Complete those items you want to, and let others slide. This is all about you.

For us, the whiteboard has been a wonderful tool to keep us honest. Part of the challenge of having so much free time is what to do with it. All too often we fall back on filling our time with activities that are related to our former lives. To combat this, we rely on our whiteboard to stimulate ideas for how best to allocate our time. For example, there was an interesting local cemetery that had been on our list and we had driven by a thousand times. When a break in our calendar allowed us the opportunity to insert a whiteboard activity, we chose to spend the day learning about this fascinating place.

Besides providing us with quick access to ideas of things to do, our whiteboard is a constant reminder of how many new and interesting things there are in the world. Checking things off a list is something that is ingrained from our work days, and it's hard to let go of. In fact, we know that we love checking things off a list. It's actually very satisfying and motivating. We'll talk later in the book about developing new metrics for success, but this is one that works for us.

In addition to keeping lists of things you want to do, now is the time to reprioritize things you have always done, but with your new life in mind. For example, we used to think about reading for pleasure as something we did before we went to bed or when we were on an airplane. And that was it.

In our new life, reading a book is something we can enjoy at every minute of every day. Maybe we do it first thing in the morning, or maybe we sit outdoors in the middle of the afternoon and read for an hour. We used to view that as a luxury that we never would give ourselves permission to do.

We have done this with several of our everyday activities that used to be "once in a while" or "only on vacation" things. We used to only watch movies in the evening or on the weekend. Now we can watch one in the morning or middle of the afternoon if we want to. We have redefined the role movies play in our lives the same way we did reading.

MILLEDGE

For many years, I wanted to be a member of a book club. I truly enjoy reading about a variety of topics and love discussing books with others. My full-time job required extensive monthly travel, but my dream was to join an interesting book club once I was in my postcareer stage. After we both sold our companies, I discovered that our postcareer travel schedule also made it a challenge. After some research, however, I found that there are many different types of virtual book clubs. I joined one and have loved being introduced to new books, learning from fellow members, and applying the learnings to my life.

We have also found that going to the movies in the middle of the day is wonderful. One time we were the only two people in the theater. We felt like royalty or the president having a private showing of the most recent blockbuster.

We have some friends who have discovered that the local theater puts on the current stage production for high school students once a month during the school day. After the performance, the actors answer questions from the crowd. It is open to the public, but very few nonstudents attend because they are working. Our friends love going to this lightly attended matinee in the middle of the week, staying to hear the actors talk about the production, and then having an early dinner afterward. It's not something they could have done during their working days, and it has become a highlight of their month.

Besides indulging in recreational activities that we used to put off, we have found that rearranging when we do everyday things can also have a very positive effect on our lives. For example, we were always getting up at 5:30 a.m. to get in our exercise before work. Now, we do it at one in the afternoon, but it took us a while to get there. When we first retired, we still would wake up early and say, "We have to go work out." And now we say, "Well, actually we don't have to do that anymore." It is a very different experience to be in a gym at six in the morning when every businessperson in the city is fighting for a treadmill and being in an empty gym at two in the middle of the afternoon. It's a much more restorative atmosphere, and one that suits our lives now.

The mantra we have begun living by is "Nothing needs to wait until a better time—you have the time right now." So far, it is serving us well.

PRIORITIZING YOURSELF GIVES YOU MORE TIME FOR OTHERS

When we talk about prioritizing ourselves, it might come off as being selfish. After all, haven't we heard our whole lives that it is better to think of others than ourselves? In reality, taking care of yourself gives you more time and energy to focus on others.

Prioritizing yourself is saying you can be in the moment in things. You don't have to bundle things up and fit them into certain times of the day or the week because your work life requires that. If your sister wants to talk, you can pick up the phone and talk. If a local charity is looking for volunteers, you can raise your hand. You have the time to take a meal to a sick friend and stay for a visit. Focusing on yourself allows you to be less selfish because you have more time to give. When we were working, we were actually pretty selfish with our time because so much of it was needed to do our jobs. Our free time was precious, and we guarded it jealously. Now we're willing to give up a lot more free time because we've eliminated a lot of unsatisfying things from our lives and have more free time to give.

MILLEDGE

Prioritizing myself has really given me the time to be present when others need help. Our nephew recently pivoted in his career and sought work in a new industry. I was able to provide real-time mentoring by talking to him before and after each interview and walking him through various scenarios, no matter what the day or time. In my previous life, if he had wanted to talk, I might have been able to find a few minutes a couple of days in the future. Now I can just say, "Call me. I'm here." Prioritizing yourself really means being in the moment. And being in the moment makes you less selfish, not more.

When we prioritize ourselves, it's not just our activities that we're prioritizing but the people we care about as well. We're doing a better job of not allowing extraneous stuff or random people to infringe on our life. When we worked, we often had to spend time with people or in places that didn't interest us, but we did it because our careers required it. Or sometimes it was just easier to say yes than no. We're being more measured about the people and things we let into our lives. We're much less forgiving about that than we used to have to be.

MOVING FORWARD

One of our friends calls this time of our lives "the gift of unstructured time." She points out that we have more unstructured time to do things with and yet at the same time, we're more conscious of an end looming out there somewhere. So you want to make sure that you're making good use of it. It's all up to you.

In our next chapter, we'll show you how being your own best friend can help you make the best use of the your newly prioritized time.

GIVE IT A TRY

- Choose a collection method (app, virtual whiteboard, or chalkboard) and start collecting ideas of interesting things that you have always wanted to do or that you hear or read about.

- The next time that you have the opportunity, choose one and give it a go!

BE YOUR OWN BEST FRIEND

Love yourself first, and everything else falls into line.

—Lucille Ball

HOW OFTEN HAVE YOU heard someone say, "I want to try something new, but I don't have anyone to do it with me"? How often have you said it yourself? Or maybe you'd like to try a new activity—drive in a road rally, take up geocaching, join an astronomy group, learn to play mah-jongg—but you just don't feel comfortable entering a new group alone. At this stage of your life, you have the time and energy to try new things, but you might not have the social network you did before, or those in your network might simply not be interested in some of the things you are. If only you had a friend you could count on to always be there for you.

You already have that perfect friend—yourself!

Think about what makes a true friend. It's someone who enjoys and embraces the same things you do. Someone who is always by your side through thick and thin. And, of course, someone who will explore new places when you want a companion for support or just company. Having a special friend to share life with just makes everything better.

However, while everyone needs to have special people in their lives, don't overlook the fact that you can have more than one friend. And one of your best can be you. Support, affirmation, and sharing can all come from within. Take this time to explore yourself, and you might be surprised by who you find.

For example, our friend Donna moved to a college town upon her retirement. She saw an advertisement for an improv class and, even though she knew no one, thought that it would be fun and interesting to enroll. When she walked into the theatre full of college-age kids, she felt awkward and out of place. However, it didn't take long for her to find her stride, and she loved the class and the students. Each class boosted her confidence that she was still the same capable, interesting person she had been during her career. She never knew that funny, assured person existed but is now determined to take her along on more outings.

BRINGING SOMETHING TO THE TABLE

When you get to this stage, you will often find that some of the things that are on your list are on your list alone. No one in your universe shares your interest or has the time to join you. And that's all right. In fact, it's better than all right. If you are going to continue to grow, you need to sometimes feel like you did something completely on your own.

PATTI

I've really enjoyed becoming a solo hiker. I go on solo hikes, and I pick something to think about while I'm hiking. Sometimes, I'll stop along the way and remember someone whom I've lost or someone that I need to repair my relationship with. When I go on these solo hikes, it's 100 percent about me. I went for a walk just two days ago, by myself, for three miles, and I listened to an incredible podcast. I didn't feel like I was alone. I felt like in the hour that I was out walking, I actually grew as a person. I gained some knowledge through listening to the podcast. I had physical exercise, I was out in the sunshine, and I was getting healthy. I said hello to a few people along the way, so I connected with other human beings. That hike was an investment in myself, and I didn't need someone else to affirm my activities.

It is our individual activities that make us unique. We certainly spend time together and with friends, but we have challenged ourselves to pursue our specific interests as well. Whether that's exploring yoga or riding a Segway.

Besides growing and expanding your interests, being your own best friend and learning things on your own makes you a better partner and friend. If you're learning new things that you can bring back to a relationship, it allows the relationship to continue to grow. We have a friend who chose to learn flower arranging by herself. She always found great joy in having a garden and fresh cut flowers in her home. She has perfected this art and finds herself arriving early for dinner parties to put the finishing touch on the centerpiece.

We all need to be able to add something interesting to the conversation—or the dinner party.

Milledge's book club, which he joined on his own, has often been a conversation starter. One recent book, *Joyful*, talks about the various things that bring joy to a person's life and how important it is to surround yourself with those things. We spent a lot of time talking about the concepts and then executed on two or three of the ideas from the book. One thing we did was add an enormous vintage Big Boy restaurant statue in our backyard, which we bought because of the inspiration from this book. We love it, and we laugh every time we see it. It makes us happy, and it is easily the one piece of art in our home that most people gravitate to. It's just a fascinating new addition to our life, and it brings us joy.

MILLEDGE

One of my ideas is to try every unique form of transportation. Although I thought that I could talk others into doing some modes of transportation with me, I knew that many would be a solo endeavor. So far, I've run a marathon (solo), zip-lined from Zambia to Zimbabwe (which I talked my lovely wife and friends into doing with me), and gone indoor skydiving (solo). When I bungee jumped off of Victoria Falls Bridge, there were no takers, but Patti and a friend spent a fabulous afternoon riding electric scooters through Paris with me. When I embarked on this challenge, I came up with more than a dozen different modes of transportation or ways of moving your body through space. I said, "I'm going to do every one of them, and if someone will do it with me, that's great. But otherwise, I'm going to do it on my own." Patti and friends did about half of them, and the rest I did on my own. It was fascinating and interesting. If I'd waited for someone else to do these things with me, it never would have happened.

It also brings joy to the people around us. Most of our visitors—friends, family, delivery drivers, caterers, landscapers—have requested a picture with the Big Boy. They also tell us stories about going to the Big Boy every year on their birthday when they were kids or having hamburgers there after Little League games or gathering at the local restaurant to celebrate special family events.

And all this joy came about because Milledge didn't wait for a friend to invite him to a book club. He joined one on his own. Being your own best friend is going on your own mission to be more joyful and saying, "I'm going to be a happier, more positive person, and it's going to make me a better partner."

A TABLE FOR ONE

If you are like us, you have spent many years surrounded by colleagues, family, and friends. Your calendar was always full. Every minute of the day was scheduled. In fact, the hours spent on airplanes were often the only time we felt we had a little time for ourselves. We used to crave alone time.

MILLEDGE

One year I ran in the New York Marathon. Even though it was going to be a solo adventure, I wanted to include others in the experience. The time from leaving my friend's apartment to the start of the race was about four hours (the same amount of time it took to run the marathon), so I decided to create a travelogue to capture each time I changed locations. So from elevator to Uber to train to ferry to bus to running the race to bike taxi home, I took a picture, added a humorous (in my mind) comment, and texted Patti (she was the bridge to everyone else). I probably sent her twenty-five texts along the way, such as "This is the next place I'm stopping," with a picture of a bus stop. Plus, I finished the race and raised $10,000 for brain cancer research. That was an awesome day!

But, truth be told, we loved the hustle and bustle. We loved being constantly among people who challenged and engaged us. It was exciting and energizing. When we stepped away from our careers, the absence of entries on our calendars was jarring. We found being alone was not as easy or attractive as we had thought.

Earlier in the chapter, we talked about how being willing to venture into new situations alone can help you stay active and expand your social networks, which is crucial if you are to continue to grow as a person. But constantly seeking out new experiences is not the only way to grow. Instead of filling empty time with activities, it is often better to allow yourself to be alone. Embrace your alone time, and reframe it as an end in its own right.

According to researchers, finding contentment and pleasure in your own company is just as important to your overall health and mental outlook as having social outlets. Those who seek out alone time are happier, feel better about their life, and experience less stress. People who enjoy alone time also appear less susceptible to depression.[9]

We have experienced these benefits ourselves. We have both found solitary activities—running, swimming, and hiking—that allow us to just be alone with our thoughts. We have become passionate about these outlets because they serve so many purposes. They keep us physically healthy—something we need to focus on more as we age—they get us outside the house, and they give us time for our thoughts and feelings to really percolate. How often have you just felt unsettled but didn't really know why? Giving yourself permission to sit quietly and meditate or go for a long walk will often give your feelings space to bubble to the surface, and you'll suddenly realize that the solution is much simpler than you thought. Authors and artists have long known that getting away to a cabin in the woods or a private studio aids their thinking. Being alone with your thoughts gives them a chance to wander—and who knows what nugget you might discover buried deep in the calm recesses of your normally on-the-go brain.

There are so many solitary activities that can bring joy—walking, reading, knitting, gardening, cooking, or watching the stars at night.

---

9   Amy Morin, "7 Science-Backed Reasons You Should Spend More Time Alone," *Forbes* online, August 5, 2017, https://www.forbes.com/sites/amymorin/2017/08/05/7-science-backed-reasons-you-should-spend-more-time-alone/#3920f9c91b7e.

Get up early and watch the sun rise. Choose one spot in your yard or the park and note how it changes as the year progresses. Write in a journal or start that book you always knew you had in you. Embrace the quiet and calm that you never had time for when you were working. Go to the gym and perfect your boxing technique. Even extroverts—maybe especially extroverts—who think they need people around them all the time to be happy will find pleasure in focusing on themselves, learning to be content with their own company, and discovering who they are as a person.

One of our friends is a corporate lawyer who is now head of a large environmental land trust. His days are almost as busy as when he was in the middle of his corporate career. He and his wife find time to travel, but every year he plans a solo, off-the-grid backpacking trip. He disconnects and just takes in the beauty of nature around him. He comes back refreshed, grounded, and ready to jump back into environmental protection issues.

Being alone does not mean you are lonely. It means you are spending time with your best friend.

Spending time alone gives you a chance to ensure there's a purpose to all the other parts of your life. Quiet space provides an opportunity to think about your goals, your progress, and changes you want to make. It gives you time to think about what really brings you joy and why. Being alone does not mean you are lonely. It means you are spending time with your best friend.

HOW TO GET STARTED

It's not always easy to change patterns of a lifetime and step out alone, but there are things you can do to make it easier.

CHANGE THE NARRATIVE

When we are afraid of doing something alone, we often picture how things can go wrong. We see ourselves being embarrassed or people ignoring us or, worse, judging us. We cognitively spin our wheels and spiral into an "I can't do that" mode. Instead of looking at the downside of doing something by yourself, change the narrative. Visualize yourself engaging in the activity alone. Go ahead and see yourself making a mistake. What happens? Instead of feeling foolish, visualize yourself laughing and feeling good about learning something new. Feel the pride of accomplishment. Studies have shown that visualization works even better if you actually spend a few minutes writing down your feelings. We can all craft our own life narrative and gain a sense of control. And with that sense of control comes confidence in our ability to do the things we want to, whether we do them alone or with others.

TAKE SMALL STEPS

When you were learning to swim, you probably did not jump into the deep end before feeling confident in your ability to handle it. Becoming comfortable doing things alone—whether it is joining in on an activity or learning to meditate—can follow much the same pattern. Have you always wanted to travel to Europe but are afraid to do it without a traveling companion? Try taking smaller trips. Maybe take a guided walking tour of your own city. Go to the museum by yourself and take advantage of the self-guided recordings. Challenge yourself to travel from one end of your city to the other using public transportation. Each time you succeed with a small step, your self-confidence grows. Put all those steps together and you'll be on your way to Europe with the only person who counts—you.

GO EASY ON YOURSELF

When self-doubt takes over, we think we must be the only ones feeling this way. (Talk about feeling alone!) In these situations, learning to practice self-compassion—and recognizing that everyone suffers from self-doubt at times—can be a much gentler and more effective road to becoming your own best friend than forcing yourself into situations you aren't ready for. The situations you are facing at this stage of life are new. There is no shame in taking things slow.

MOVING FORWARD

When we were working, most of us were experiencing new and thought-provoking things on a daily basis. We were well-read and well-informed, interesting and interested, and that led to feeling confident and engaged. You don't need to leave that behind at this stage of life. Just grab that best friend—who always wants to do exactly what you want to do—and go to the ballet, the antique car rally, the wine-tasting experience, or whatever else grabs your fancy. You'll never want to use the excuse "I have no one to go with" again.

When you get to this point, you are ready to go on to the next chapter on finding your passions, which will be easier because you've already found yourself.

GIVE IT A TRY

- Make a list of ten things that you have always wanted to do.

- Put a star by two of them that you would be willing to do alone, and give them a try.

- Integrate your solo experience into your relationships by sharing them with others.

RESOLUTION 5

FIND YOUR PASSION

It's never too late to be what you might have been.

—George Elliot

NOW THAT WE'VE worked our way through becoming our own best friend, it's time to put that knowledge into action. We all have a superpower, something that underpinned our success during our careers and can now be targeted for good in our Resolutionist life. The trick is to find your passions and apply that superpower. Some passions have probably been part of your life forever. Others sneak up on us.

Cathryn (superpower—*action*) likes to say that she never went looking for her passion—it came looking for her. Not long after she left her corporate life as a public relations expert, one of her neighbors knocked on her door and asked if she would accompany her to a fundraiser for a local art gallery. Cathryn wasn't familiar with this particular gallery but appreciated the invitation. She had no idea there was so much talent in the neighborhoods around her. The next morning Cathryn thought about how this experience resonated with her and decided to get involved. She began researching the local artists and offered pro bono PR services to raise their profile. She joined the board of the art gallery, as well as the board of the larger museum in town, where she lobbied for more local representation. Cathryn spent more than thirty years refining her superpower and is now using it to embrace her passion.

THE MANY FACES OF PASSION

In many cases, the things that satisfy our soul were set aside while our careers were the priority. We were being paid to perform a job that rarely involved our own passions. Now that we have stepped away from the structure and demands of a busy career, we can focus on the things that make our lives meaningful. In this stage of our lives, we haven't stopped working. We have added more meaning to the work that we are doing.

We haven't stopped working. We have added more meaning to the work that we are doing.

Participating in activities that bring us joy and fulfillment has been shown to have both psychological and physical benefits. Engaging in activities that bring meaning to our lives can improve moods, well-being, and life satisfaction, as well as encouraging fewer depressed moods, less stress and/or more stress-coping strategies, and better cardiovascular health. A 2015 Society for Behavioral Health study found that participants who engaged in satisfying personal activities were 34 percent less stressed and 18 percent less sad during the activities, as well as for some time after.[10] These activities could be anything from sitting on a charity board to fostering kittens. The theme that linked them was that the study participants were engaging in the activities that drove measurable improvement in their life.

MILLEDGE

As I was considering my move to the next phase of life, I could not point to a passion that I knew would consume me. I did, however, have a list of many hobbies, activities, charities, educational opportunities, and travels to get started. It was a process of experimentation to help me find passions that would drive me. For example, I did not know which nonprofit would capture my enthusiasm until I found Soles4Souls. Their mission of "wearing out poverty" and focus on improving people's lives through microenterprise struck a nerve. It is obvious that Soles4Souls is making the world a better place and that, using the resources from my career, I can help the organization. I truly found a passion where the skills from my previous career could help.

---

10   Matthew J. Zawadzki, Joshua M. Smyth, and Heather J. Costigan, "Real-Time Associations Between Engaging in Leisure and Daily Health and Well-Being," The Society of Behavioral Medicine, February 28, 2015, https://www.ucmerced.edu/sites/ucmerced.edu/files/documents/zawadzki-paper-2015.pdf.

PASSIONS CAN BE "RIGHT-SIZED"

The word "passion" evokes an image of something big, important, earth-shattering. But passions are really anything that increase your happiness and inspire you to get out of bed each morning. Maybe you have a passion for baking and want to spend more time perfecting breads from around the world or just more time smelling luscious aromas in your kitchen. Maybe you are a film buff, and now you have time to take classes and travel to festivals or simply watch more films.

We have another friend (superpower—*empathy*) who, after acquiring a law degree from Oxford, listened to her compassionate self and chose a career in human resources, eventually leading the HR effort at a leading software company. She has always had the confidence to be in touch with her soft side—tending to the needs of scores of employees over many years. She was also committed to animal welfare and the treatment of our furry friends. Upon retirement she took some time to enjoy life and once settled dedicated herself and her time to shining a light on animal welfare. She joined the board of her local Humane Society and now has assumed the role of chair of the charity's board. She is using her well-honed skills and experience to advance a cause that she has a passion for—and she always has a few adorable adopted kittens to love!

Others might want to go big and engage in passions that take most of their time, such as becoming a full-time college professor, running for political office, or working as a CEO-for-hire on a contract basis. The point is that the size or amount of time involved does not make one passion more important or more credible than another. A passion is anything that makes you feel happier and more alive.

PATTI

For me, it's really been more about my passions finding me. My passion is to make a difference. Right now I'm focused on the sport of soccer and the Conservatory Theater in San Francisco. I developed an interest in soccer when we lived in London, and I really missed it when we returned home. One day, after we returned to the States, I was having lunch with a business associate, and I shared this with him. He encouraged me to convert my "love of the game" into action … and I did. Serving the US Soccer Community as a board trustee has been a wonderful experience. However, it's possible that over time my interests may pivot. Maybe I will find myself making a difference in childhood education or in health and wellness or childhood obesity. If I apply myself to a situation and we move it to the next stage, it may be time for me to move to something else that inspires me. I am in search of those niche places where my corporate skills and experience can help to move an organization forward.

Many take up writing, painting, or other creative passions during this stage of life. They now have the time to indulge a side of themselves that they had to push aside during their career years. They can finally spend as much time on the things that interest them most.

PASSIONS CAN BE OTHERS-FOCUSED

This is a time when people dive deeper into philanthropic endeavors. They have probably been generous with donations in the past but now they can be more engaged. We know one couple (superpowers—*persuasiveness and enthusiasm*) who have always donated generously to environmental causes, as well as groups that work to help young women rise out of poverty. Now that they have more time, they have both taken on leadership roles in prominent and active philanthropic organizations, as well as becoming more involved with their family foundation.

While there are certainly more passions in life than philanthropy, this is often the time when people who have an excess of time, energy, and money look to give back. When we left the corporate world, we established the Hart Family Foundation to fund and support our interests. This gave us a structure to support things like performing arts, the world of international soccer, and poverty eradication. Whether you have a passion for social rights or human rights, education, or the homeless problem, one of the tools that you might want in your toolbox is a funding mechanism.

Philanthropic giving—time, money, goods, energy, and ideas—is not just for the wealthy. The charitable world needs gifts large and small to carry out their mission. Everybody has something to give, and your generosity will be welcomed by organizations in need of your donation. Once you find your passions, the returns are rewarding and the fuel that you are providing will change lives.

Many of us are interested in impact investing. We want to use our skills and knowledge to further the cause. One couple we know has always been generous with their resources, and even started a family foundation to help select charities. He was interested in alleviating hunger, while she was more focused on education. As they began to step away from their company, they were able to ramp up their personal involvement in their passions. He is now the chair of a large nonprofit that oversees national food banks, while she is a board trustee for her alma mater. They have also redirected their foundation to provide business advice and best-in-class processes in addition to financial support.

Passion can't just be a free-floating feeling. To work, at least for this generation, it needs to be focused and there needs to be measurable results. The number one guiding principle for our family foundation is engaged giving. We're not only giving financially but also giving our time, our energy, and our expertise. When we seek out opportunities to make a difference, we do so in an engaged manner. Most of us have worked very hard for the donations we are making and think responsibly about how we put our resources to work to make the world a better place.

KEEP SEARCHING UNTIL YOU ARE HAPPY

For people who pride themselves on following through with commitments, it can be hard to step away from something we thought we should be passionate about. Give yourself space to find the right fit instead of staying with something that isn't quite right. Give yourself permission to try a variety of activities before finding the perfect outlet for your skills and energy.

Brenda (superpower—*determination*) spent her entire professional life rising to the top of a male-dominated industry. When she handed her C-suite key to her successor, she was way overdue for some rest and relaxation. Soon she realized that she needed a new plan to invigorate her life. She always enjoyed being a strategic thinker so she thought entering the corporate boardroom would be the perfect blend of her superpower and her interests. After attending a prestigious women's director development program, she realized that serving investors from the boardroom was not her "cup of tea." She pivoted and founded an organization that provides support, training, and scholarships for young women as they progress to the executive ranks of industrial companies. She speaks at conferences and universities and is now mentoring the next generation of female leaders. Giving herself permission to change course has allowed Brenda to find her true passion.

> **Life isn't just a basic box of eight crayons; it's a huge box of many different colors.**

Feel free to engage in multiple passions. The right ones will rise to the top. Your interests and passions will change over the years. Go with it. Life isn't just a basic box of eight crayons; it's a huge box of many different colors. Feel free to sample each one before choosing your favorites.

MANY PASSIONS MAKE A WHOLE

Something we have noticed as we've built a postcareer network is that people often think they can only have one passion in their life. They will focus all of their energy on environmental issues or rehabbing historical houses or becoming involved in politics. Everything else is something lesser. We call this resolution "Find Your Passion," but for many people, including us, life is full of passions. If you live your life with tunnel vision, you may easily miss opportunities just out of sight. But if you greet each day with your eyes wide open, you will often become aware of passions you didn't know you had.

Nancy (superpower—*confidence*) has been passionate her entire adult life about helping women succeed. While working, she often mentored younger women and helped them up the ladder. Once "retired," she began to look for areas where she could make a difference. She likes to say that when she was working, she had a very narrow focus. Now she has the ability to open the lens wider. Because she is a lawyer, she began looking at criminal justice issues and where the system most often failed the most vulnerable people, particularly women. Her goal was to help organizations serving this population become more robust. Now this is where passions can overlap. She loves to travel. So she traveled with groups to India, to Cambodia, to Vietnam, to Guatemala, and to other places that intrigued her. While in each of these countries, she also looked at what they were doing to alleviate poverty. She saw how microfinance and the efficient use of limited resources could completely change the trajectory of a person's life. She came home and dove into helping local organizations make the most efficient and impactful use of their resources.

Jeremy (superpower—*adventurousness*) loves to cook. He pairs this passion with his love of travel and history. He and his wife will choose countries to travel to based on their interest in history. As they explore the various regions, he will make it a point to sample as many local dishes as possible. When he gets home, he happily spends time in the kitchen as he tries to recreate some of his favorites.

At this stage you have permission to allow multiple things to move forward, as opposed to one thing. You also have the ability to pick and choose your preferred topic. It's not unusual for someone to enthusiastically embrace an activity, only to find their interest wanes as circumstances change. Agreeing to engage with an organization is not a lifetime commitment. You can enjoy the activity and, when or if circumstances change, move on to something new.

One part of our life focuses on using our skills to help nonprofits become more successful. Another is our passion for travel. We see travel as a proxy for continuing education. Even though we traveled a tremendous amount during our careers, we have focused on a more comprehensive travel experience in this phase of our lives. We try to stay long enough in a place to learn about the local customs and some of the things that make this location unique, so it's not just a typical tourist excursion. We know a couple who spend at least three months every year living in a different country. Before they go, they familiarize themselves with the traditions, culture, and language. Then they immerse themselves in the local community. Their passion is to truly understand cultures different from their own, and they are doing it through spending a significant amount of time in each locale.

We have also become dedicated to improving our health. Our daily routines include swimming, hiking, and running. But we also are doing a number of other things that test what makes us feel better, whether it's around sleep, food, meditation, or exercise. We consider this part of the "passion" category because we're spending a lot of time, energy, and effort to help ourselves move forward and feel better.

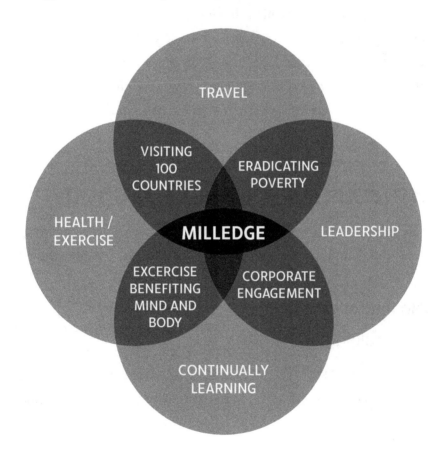

Multiple passions can actually be visualized with a Venn diagram, where each is a circle. These circles will overlap around a core set of skills or interests that drive you to embrace each individually. The overlap of these circles is where you will find the whole person, one who is interested and interesting and one who is still growing and fulfilled. Milledge's involvement in Soles4Souls is the perfect example. He has a drive to eradicate poverty and found a group that resonates with that objective. While working with this group, he often visits other countries (travel), where he spends a significant amount of time exploring the region on foot (exercise) and learning about the culture (continually learning).

Passions can be anything that energizes you: sailing, gardening, bird-watching, auto racing, yoga, or genealogy. The things that bring you the most joy fit into the passion category. The wonderful thing about "retirement" is that we not only have the time to try different passions on for size, but we also have the time to indulge in as many of them as we like.

USE YOUR SUPERPOWER FOR GOOD

Life is full of transitions and stages. Through it all, you undoubtedly have found an inner strength or character trait that has allowed you to thrive. Maybe you approach the world with an optimism that helps you remain positive, no matter what the challenge. Maybe you are persistent and just keep going when others give up. Maybe you can quickly find solutions to problems or are able to put others at ease. No matter what it is, applying your superpower to your passions will multiply the good you do—and the good you feel.

> **No matter what it is, applying your superpower to your passions will multiply the good you do.**

PATTI

My superpower is *courage*. Courage to go first, to be the only; courage to be alone in my quest for a better life. Being courageous in the face of adversity— winning against the odds and taking the risk required to achieve my dreams has been my "go-to" characteristic. As a woman coming up in the business world, courage was required. Blazing your own trail was the only option. To be the one woman, wife, mom in almost every situation meant rules didn't exist and expectations were not well defined. Being successful in spite of the ambiguity required me to live my life boldly and confidently. Courage was a constant—and quite essential.

Thinking about your superpower can help you winnow the possibilities of ways to spend your time. There are just an incredible number of paths to take or areas to support—arts, sports, poverty, education, health, animals, environment; this list obviously goes on and on. So when you look at these opportunities to engage and are feeling a little overwhelmed, it sometimes helps to stop and say, "What is my superpower?" What was it when you were working? If you come across an area of interest, activity, charity, or any situation that you think you might like to embrace, ask if applying your superpower would elicit better results. If so, this might be a really good fit. If not, you might want to ask if this interest is really something you are going to feel passionate about.

MILLEDGE

My superpower is *discipline*. Having grown up in a very structured environment, being disciplined comes naturally to me. From an early age, I believed in setting measurable goals as a way to focus on improving. This discipline served me well as an investment banker, and I'm now turning it toward nonprofit work, where success is sometimes measured differently. However, when it comes to spending limited capital to have the largest impact, I believe these organizations can often benefit from a more businesslike discipline. Everyone wants to make sure the limited funds are used wisely, and I think I can help with that.

MOVING FORWARD

Complacency is the kryptonite of superpowers. In other words, the more you use your superpower, the stronger it will become and the more impact you will have in this new phase of your life.

GIVE IT A TRY

- Identify your superpower. If you are unsure, ask a friend or family member.

- Make a list of those things that you are passionate about.

- Prioritize your list.

- Rely on your superpower to advance your passion!

- Extra credit: Create your personal Venn diagram.

DEVELOP YOUR ELEVATOR PITCH

If you can't explain it simply, you don't understand it well enough.

—Albert Einstein

A FEW YEARS AGO, we took an international trip with several other couples. They were all Resolutionists with very interesting lives, past and present. The first night we were getting to know each other, and almost without fail, everyone was talking about what they *used* to do. They mentioned their careers, the places they had lived, and the universities they attended. What wasn't in the conversation was what they were doing *then*. Throughout our journey, we continued to debate as a group the merits of our "illustrious pasts" against the activities that presently filled our schedules. We decided to dedicate an entire dinner conversation to pushing each individual through the threshold to a new elevator pitch. We learned many enlightening things about one another: "I am restoring my mother's wedding dress for my daughter to wear when she marries," "I am hiking numerous religious pilgrimages," "I am working to legalize graffiti art in a blighted area of my city"—all things that were worth sharing and were windows into the hearts and souls of our fellow travelers.

Looking at yourself in the rearview mirror is much too common at this stage of our lives. Our careers gave us a sense of identity and a narrative that made it easier for people to understand us. But if you were still working, you wouldn't define yourself by what you were doing three jobs ago. You'd tell people about your current role. We should be doing the same thing when we move beyond our professional lives.

Once we enter the Resolutionist stage, it is time to redefine our identity to reflect what we are doing now. Step away from what has given you your self-worth and confidence for most of your adult life, and find that same self-worth in this new life. When someone asks, "What are you doing?" create a story for what you are doing today: "I am restoring an old historic home." Or "I am reading Amazon's 100 Books to Read in a Lifetime." Or "I am working to shift the conversation about racism in our country." Whatever you decide, it will be more relevant than defining yourself by your past.

The idea of an elevator pitch developed following numerous social events where we found ourselves rehashing the things we had previously accomplished but not articulating what was important to us at that point. So if we want to make true and deeper connections, we have to be open to sharing those things that we are dedicated to now.

MILLEDGE

If your elevator pitch is around what you're doing right now or what you're hoping to achieve, it changes the conversation from what you did in the past—"Oh, what did you do when you were an investment banker and what kind of deals did you work on?"—to what you are doing now. What you are doing now is likely more interesting and engaging than your previous career. For example, my elevator pitch right now is "I'm currently focused on three different organizations where I'm chairman: an investment bank, an oil and gas distribution company, and a nonprofit that's eradicating poverty. I'm close to my lifetime goal of visiting a hundred countries, and I'm writing a book." This gives almost anyone fodder to ask questions about the things that are current and important to me. My enthusiasm is likely to come through during my pitch, and that alone tends to make a conversation better.

Take pride in your current activities and contributions. Even if your historic elevator pitch didn't include nonprofit exploits or bucket list items, these are relevant to you now and will be interesting to others. If you speak with fervor about these activities, others will be intrigued.

We decided to shift from revisiting our past to shining a light on our current selves. Both of us developed a brief description that we use to introduce ourselves when we make new acquaintances. We find that these introductory conversations are more often leading to new friendships. Basing your relationships on those things that are presently occupying your mind and calendar enhances the opportunity to stay connected over the long term.

PATTI

I remember the time Milledge and I were at an event and it started out with everyone saying something about themselves. There was a gentleman in the group who was recently retired. When it got to him, he said, "What am I? I don't really know." It turned into an interesting conversation. I realized that I was coming away from these gatherings not feeling very good about myself. We were spending the entire time talking about the industries that I had worked in when I was working full-time. We were spending no time talking about the arts community or setting up foundations or global soccer. The people in the room didn't know we should be talking about those things because I hadn't told them. I wasn't really exposing the current me to the audience. Milledge and I decided that we needed an elevator pitch that included what we're doing now so that we could change the conversation. We have found that synthesizing what we are doing now into two or three sentences has an enormous impact on your self-confidence. When you're spending all your time with others going down memory lane versus talking about the inspirational things you've done this week, it makes you ask, "Have I left the best of me behind?" when, in fact, you haven't.

We never knew so many people were interested in soccer, and we have had great conversations about the soccer universe. We have great conversations with people about setting up foundations, evaluating new investments, and our various nonprofit interests. Saying that you are consolidating an industry for a family-owned business is a surefire way to pique people's interest. Someone is bound to say, "Wow! What does that even mean? How do you do that?" And the conversation is off and running.

We are passionate about travel. When we say we're approaching our lifetime goal of visiting one hundred countries, it naturally leads to questions such as "Where is the last place you went?" "What's next on your list?" "How do you select the countries you visit?" It opens up new and interesting conversations because you're trading real-time information. Someone else might have just come back from Vietnam or Iceland or Botswana. Soon, everyone is comparing their favorite countries, which ones they'd visit again and which ones they'd recommend. The conversations become much more productive and engaging and lead to actions that enhance your life now.

KEEP IT REAL

The process of describing yourself to others is an ongoing exercise. Your life is not static, so your pitch isn't either. When you were working, it's likely your elevator pitch stayed the same for years. But this stage of your life is actually very dynamic. You are probably going in and out of activities and in and out of different causes. As you drop some interests and pick up others, you will want to adjust your self-descriptions to match your current life.

Our elevator pitches today look very different than they did originally. We've done numerous iterations because it has taken time to get the formula right. Some feel it needs to be impressive. It doesn't. We are who we are, and all have a dimension that others will find appealing. The key is to be honest and unapologetic and to capture this moment in your life.

One real advantage of having an elevator pitch is that it gives you the confidence to enter any situation. Earlier we talked about getting comfortable with the uncomfortable and being willing to do things by yourself. Being prepared with your story makes entering unfamiliar situations much easier.

MOVING FORWARD

Coming up with two or three sentences that describe what you are doing now and invite people to engage with you shouldn't be that hard—but it often is. People aren't used to thinking about their everyday lives in the same way they did their work lives. We've spent decades separating business from personal, and that often had the result of people thinking their personal lives were not very important or interesting. What you did at work was what made you important and interesting. Now you need to reset your thinking. Change the narrative. Be proud of what you do because it brings you happiness. If you are excited by what you do, others will be as well.

> The things you add to your list do not need to be huge, monumental, or far-reaching. Right now, we are watching all the James Bond movies in chronological order and have added that to our elevator pitch.

The things you add to your list do not need to be huge, monumental, or far-reaching. Right now, we are watching all the James Bond movies in chronological order and have added that to our elevator pitch. People love debating which movies they liked the most, or the merits of Sean Connery versus Roger Moore versus Daniel Craig. This is the type of conversation that is relevant to how we are spending our time and provides a connection to other people.

GIVE IT A TRY

- Write an elevator pitch that shares your current activities, interests, and aspirations.

- Feel free to seek input from your kindred spirits.

- Try it the next time you need to introduce yourself.

- Refine it, incorporate it into your life, and be prepared to modify it as you evolve.

CAN YOU GUESS WHO THESE PEOPLE ARE BASED ON THEIR ELEVATOR PITCHES?

1. Since leaving my government job, I've spent forty years overseeing my family's agriculture business, as well as teaching Sunday school and building houses for Habitat for Humanity. During these four decades, I have thrown myself into the mission of my center—advancing human rights and alleviating human suffering—as well as using my skills for diplomatic missions. I'd love to talk to you about how we can bring countries together peacefully or the best hammer to use when putting up sheetrock.

2. I spent my career in and around the NBA, first as a player, then in a series of administrative jobs for various franchises, and finally as a TV commentator. I had ten surgeries during my pro career and ended up abusing prescription drugs for more than fifteen years. I almost lost everything, but with lots of support, I was able to beat the addiction. Now my passion is helping at-risk youth avoid opioid addition, as well as restoring people's faith in their fellow man through funny and feel-good videos on my Twitter feed. Want to see a video of a weatherman broadcasting from home and trying unsuccessfully to control his dog?

3. My previous career was spent in government. I served several presidents and held positions ranging from consumer affairs advisor to secretary of labor and transportation. I was elected senator from my state, and even tested the waters for a presidential race. But through all of this, one of my favorite jobs was president of the American Red

Cross. Now I'm back to doing what I love—providing real help to people. My Hidden Heroes Foundation provides support for those taking care of our military veterans.

4. I spent my career as CEO of a tech firm, but now I find satisfaction using my wealth to run a global foundation focused on empowering the poorest in the world to transform their lives through access to healthcare, training, education, and financial resources. Let's talk about how much better life is around the world today than it was fifty years ago.

5. Medical issues forced me to step away from my NBA career, but it was really a blessing in disguise. I've spent the past twenty-five years working to revitalize urban areas by investing in retail development, such as Starbucks, movie theaters, and restaurants, in neighborhoods that other commercial estate developers are ignoring. I've got some great stories of choosing the right locations.

6. I'm a pro at transitioning to new phases of life. I've been a professional body builder, model, and successful businessman, as well as an A-list movie star. In a twist no one saw coming, I was elected governor of California. Politics wasn't a passion, but as a businessman, I recognized it was one of the best ways to set my ideas into motion. Today, I'm able to use my business and acting skills to promote green energy, electric cars, and the benefits of staying fit in person and on my YouTube channel. The video where I'm an undercover used car salesman promoting electric cars should be nominated for an Oscar.

7. I loved singing professionally, and my soulful love songs are pretty well known, but these days I prefer being a preacher at a small church in Tennessee. Let's go do some karaoke.

8. I spent most of my life in the movies. In fact, I started so young that I wouldn't call it a career choice. When I finally left the business, I was able to do what I really wanted to do—serve as a diplomat around the world. I was a delegate to the UN, a US ambassador to more than one country, and the first female chief of protocol of the United States. I have some wonderful stories.

9. In our previous life, we were Yale-educated attorneys working in both New York and Paris. But our love of food brought us to our second career—overseeing a survey that allows diners to rate restaurants so that others can find the best ones in a city. What's your favorite restaurant?

10. It's hard to beat being an astronaut, but I really feel I'm doing more important work as the senator from Ohio. I'm able to truly make a difference in people's lives by representing their interests in Congress, as well as use my problem-solving superpower to attack some of the nation's hardest problems.

11. I spent decades singing both onstage and on television, but when it was time to step away from that career, I found I had a passion for politics. I have a talent for connecting with large audiences, and I am able to use that talent to generate enthusiasm for my campaign. I love representing my constituents in Congress and watching out for their interests.

ANSWERS

1. President Jimmy Carter

2. Rex Chapman

3. Senator Elizabeth Dole

4. Bill Gates

5. Magic Johnson

6. Governor Arnold Schwarzenegger

7. Al Green

8. Ambassador Shirley Temple Black

9. Tina and Tim Zagat

10. Senator John Glenn

11. Representative Sonny Bono

RESOLUTION 7

ENGAGE YOUR RESOURCES

Now is no time to think of what you do not have.
Think of what you can do with what there is.

—Ernest Hemingway

ONE OF OUR GOALS entering this phase of life was to author a book together. We imagined it would bring us closer together and refine our approach to "retirement." However, we aren't writers and quickly realized that to successfully achieve our goal, we would need to engage our resources. We approached our friends and associates who had previously written books and asked them to share their experiences, good and not so good. We learned a few tricks of the trade and had the great fortune of benefiting from others' missteps. We asked for introductions to potential publishers and chose one with a publishing model that suited our style. Leaning on those with legal experience, we solicited assistance with the contractual process and put ourselves in the hands of experts. We engaged our very kind friends and associates, who lent their stories to this book—it is their experiences that have made the pages of *The Resolutionist* come to life. Of course, we also contributed our financial resources to realize our dream, but it was a virtual community that made this dream a reality.

As professionals, most of us have learned to be resourceful throughout our careers, including the use of industry contacts, information, and support staff, as well as our own skill set and institutional knowledge. It was second nature to access whatever we needed to solve a problem or answer a question. Today, we can use the same strategy to promote and move our passions forward.

For example, if you have taken on a leadership role in a nonprofit, you might use your own knowledge of managerial best practices to help streamline the reporting structure. Maybe your ability to read and analyze data would help the organization become more efficient. You probably have people in your network who could volunteer time and knowledge to enhance the mission. Or one of your contacts may have access to a venue or entertainment for the annual fundraiser. The resources we have access to help us live our best lives—and it is up to us to make sure they are used wisely.

MILLEDGE & PATTI

We always thought about "engaging our resources" as something that was strictly business oriented. Utilizing the multitude of assets that we had created or earned was a reasonable path forward. As with many things, however, it took some fellow Resolutionists to shed light on a new way to think about our resources. Our friends Toni and Ed have always encouraged us to add new perspectives to our lives. We find our discussions with them over lunch or a drink broaden our view of the world. They shared with us a tradition that we have found to be a micro approach to engaging your resources. We own several large boxes of greeting cards that we have exchanged over the years—each chosen carefully and the messages written with great intention. We add to our "stash" every year—Mother's Day, Father's Day, Valentine's Day, anniversaries, birthdays, Easter, Halloween, Christmas, thank you, congratulations, and every other possible celebration. Toni and Ed suggested that we look at these treasures as "resources to engage," and we did! We go to the box of cards and reuse them, and we have found great satisfaction in recycling our past greetings. It is a real adventure to choose the right card, add a new message—and read the old message as well. We are still acknowledging all of the special moments in our lives but doing so in a much more eco-friendly fashion—and in fact, combining a walk down memory lane with a current event. Thank you to the Sarrailles— you are true Resolutionists!

DIVE INTO YOUR NEW JOB

The more attention you give to your assets, the more robust and relevant they will be. Tending to your resources is now *job one*! Just as an investment portfolio or social network will shrivel and die if not actively managed, so too will your personal environment. Our focus has shifted from efficiently managing our employer's resources to making certain that we are managing our own—time, energy, finances—to the best of our ability. The time is now to take the reins of our personal "treasures." Be purposeful in how they are allocated, and challenge yourself to make certain that they grow and prosper.

Let's get started! Define your current state. This may sound simple, but we found it to be quite time-consuming. This is the perfect opportunity to borrow processes and procedures from your professional career. This will allow you to clearly see areas for improvement in the personal management of your resources. We took a look at every nook and cranny of our lives. We reviewed credit card statements to know where we were spending our money. We also looked at the cards themselves to be certain the benefits were either being used or were the right benefits for us. We introduced ourselves to all the frequent flyer and other traveler programs to remind ourselves of the redemption levels and restrictions and put together a plan to integrate these into our future travel. Next were our insurance policies (health, auto, homeowners, liability) and estate plans. Were they appropriate for our lives now, or were there changes that needed to be made? Did we still need life insurance, and were adjustments in our deductibles for auto and health appropriate? A comprehensive look at our investment portfolio was absolutely necessary to determine if we were still investing for the long term or our horizons had changed. Are we generating enough income to cover our expenses? Another question was "How many subscriptions does a family need?" We reviewed and consolidated all of our magazine, newspaper, phone, and content subscriptions to optimize for this phase of our life. How about service providers? From our cable television company to our tax accountant to the local teenager who mowed our lawn, we reviewed all to determine what we could do ourselves and what we would continue to outsource. If we continued to outsource, were we using the right partner? We realized that we were doing many things because they had always been done that way and, frankly, we hadn't prioritized our time to eliminate inefficiencies. But now we were able to apply our abundant resource of time to review, assess, and adjust. This entire process took several months, but we found ourselves with simpler, more efficient arrangements as a result.

One of the unintended benefits of this exercise is the increased self-sufficiency with which we live our lives. There was a great swath of activity that we could do ourselves that allowed us to develop new skills and has reduced the complexity of many tasks. Learning how to do things for yourself doesn't have to be on-the-job training. Every community has continuing education classes that teach the ins and outs of personal finance, investing, and computers. You will also find classes on gardening, landscaping, decorating, and just about any other activity you can think of. Your local hardware store likely offers classes on home repair, plumbing, tiling, and general renovation skills. Don't feel pressured to take on more than you want to—we gave up that type of pressure when we left the workforce—but if you have an interest in taking on more of the things you've asked others to do in the past, there are lots of support services to get you there.

We also have a list of less important items that we are working our way through, such as photographing and creating an inventory of our jewelry and other valuables and organizing twenty years' worth of photos of our life. Organizing your music collection, books, and important papers would also fit into this category. Once organized, these assets can become a resource that enhances your life. Looking through old pictures while listening to the perfect music mix can bring real joy.

With the basics behind us, we decided to delve into the relation-ships in our lives and decide where to apply resources to strengthen our bonds with other human beings. For many years, we traveled, dined, and built memories with business associates. Now it was up to us to choose those that we wanted to include on our life journey and to bolster ties with our family and those that we had neglected during our climb up the corporate ladder. We set out to deepen relationships where there were common interests and have found that our social network has become one of our most valuable resources.

With so many dimensions of our life now organized and prioritized, we were able to direct surplus resources (time, energy, creativity, money) to external causes. Making time to commit to charitable organizations has provided great affirmation to both of us. Giving the gift of yourself is a most rewarding act. The outward application of our life's experience through mentoring others has returned to us a hundredfold.

TIME IS YOUR MOST VALUABLE RESOURCE

Using your time wisely is the most impactful thing you can do to augment your life. Your time is a currency. Your time has value. Stephen Covey, the author of *The 7 Habits of Highly Effective People*, points out that you can spend time on a myriad of things, but if you call the use of time "investing," you are more likely to invest your time in something that has value and importance for you rather than squander it. Thus, choose your goals wisely so that time you spend on them becomes an investment, not an expense.

When we first started reviewing our situation, we found that we were often spending our time unwisely, whether it was waiting around for a service person to arrive or doing things we really didn't want to do. Developing a management system that included looking for efficient investments in time has made our life exponentially better.

MILLEDGE

It seems counterintuitive, but I am more aware of how I spend my time now than I ever was during my days in the workforce. My life moves vertically from high stakes to low stakes more than it used to do because I have the ability to indulge in more interests. When I was at work, my life pretty much stayed at one broad, horizontal level. But now I might be working on my investments, doing Zoom calls on one of my boards, and then stop to make sure the hummingbird feeder is full. I might return to my home office and work a bit on the nonprofit I chair, then take another break to get in a workout. Being able to enjoy a full range of activities is what make my life full and enjoyable.

Time management does not mean rigorously blocking out every minute of the day—unless you're the type of person that somehow gets comfort from that structure. For most people, it is just setting goals and priorities, then making sure you plan for how you are going to accomplish them. It is being productive with your time.

To be productive, it helps to put yourself back into the mindset you had at work. Managing yourself is, after all, your new job.

To be productive, it helps to put yourself back into the mindset you had at work. Managing yourself is, after all, your new job. That generally begins with having a space in the house that serves as your home office. It's nice if it is a true home office in a designated room, but the dining room table or breakfast bar can work just as well. In addition to a specific workspace, we have found having a specific time when we review our household workings and finances, as well as progress toward various goals, makes us more focused and efficient. It helps us drill down on the tasks at hand and gets us in the right mindset to view running our household in the same way we ran our businesses.

The idea behind a time-management system at this stage of our lives is it creates a consistent structure, which is something that we relied on during our successful careers. Some of the strategies you can use to incorporate time management into your routines include:

USE A CALENDAR

After you have worked decades in corporations, scheduling events on a calendar is second nature. There is no reason to stop now. Just as calendars helped you manage your corporate obligations, they can help you organize yourself now. Too often people just think they will remember that they have yoga on Tuesday and Thursday and volunteer at the local animal shelter on Wednesday. But then they begin adding a lunch here or a board meeting there and pretty soon find themselves scurrying from activity to activity, and it all gets overwhelming. Looking at a calendar each day gives us an idea of how our life is progressing and lets us know if we need to make adjustments—either pulling back because we have committed to too much or adding things because we are letting life pass us by. And in today's world of digital calendars and meeting invites, it could not be simpler.

MAKE A DAILY LIST

Some people are planners and make lists for everything, but even those who like to let life just happen will often find making to-do lists helpful in assuring that nothing gets forgotten. Be flexible, however. The list is to help keep you on track, but if you'd rather do something else today, always feel free to move items to another time. Just make a new list—or simply skip them altogether if you discover you really don't want to do them. There is not a right or wrong way. We use a digital shared list system, but some of our friends use sticky notes very effectively.

TREAT EVERYTHING LIKE A BUSINESS APPOINTMENT

Give yourself permission to enter items in your calendar or to-do list that historically you wouldn't. Thirty minutes for meditation or an hour to read a book or an afternoon to try a new recipe. These are your preferred "appointments" now and are equal in importance to board meetings or conference calls.

ADAPT YOUR SYSTEM AS YOUR NEEDS CHANGE

Some people begin "retirement" doing all the things they'd been putting off because they never had the time, such as redecorating the living room, traveling, or playing golf every day. But that first burst of activity usually begins to wear, and you realize you want more from this stage. At that point it makes sense to reevaluate your resources and goals. Be aware of how you feel about certain activities and be ready to drop some and pick up others as your time and interests change.

MOVING FORWARD

You have spent a lifetime cultivating, creating, and consolidating resources that can now be used to make this stage of life the best ever. Your network, battle scars, wealth, knowledge, wisdom, know-how, time (the most valuable of all), and your reputation all allow you to contribute to your own personal happiness, as well as the success of the organizations that you support. Managing and embracing these resources becomes the focus of your life—expanding them, applying them, nurturing them—this is the icing on top of a very lovely cake!

Just as making good financial investments provides you with additional capital, investing your time wisely provides you with more time to do things you really want to do, and that will make your life so much better. Because we have organized our resources to function efficiently, we have time to spend on things that weren't priorities before. We go to farmers markets more. We cook at home more. We care about the garden and the hummingbirds. Just sitting on the patio watching the hummingbirds was never on our radar before. But now it is, and we love it.

And that's the bottom line. Bringing order to your life gives you the time you need to stop and smell the roses or volunteer at your local food bank.

But our lives can be much more. Come with us to the next chapter, as we talk about how to convert dreams to reality. Now that you have your life organized, you will certainly have the time!

GIVE IT A TRY

- Make a list of the top three resources that you have accumulated during your career.

- Identify something in your life that needs resolution.

- Apply the resources at your disposal to bring this situation to closure.

DREAM LESS AND DO MORE

All our dreams can come true, if we have the courage to pursue them.

—Walt Disney

SHERRIE AND KARL dream of taking each of their grandchildren on an African safari before they enter college. To make that dream come true, however, it will take more than magical thinking. It will take years of planning. Their current grandchildren range in age from three to ten, and it is likely more will follow. To make this long-term goal a reality, Sherrie and Karl have designed a short-term action plan that will lead to several future African safaris.

STEP 1: Tend to health, wellness, fitness, and diet, allowing them to endure the physical requirements of a safari.

STEP 2: Strengthen relationships with their children and grand-children, creating the opportunity for an enjoyable and stress-free family vacation.

STEP 3: Invest wisely to ensure that there are adequate resources to fund the dream of a lifetime.

Who hasn't sat at their desk daydreaming of running away to spend the rest of their life on an exotic island? Those dreams serve a purpose, but they aren't typically dreams we expect to fulfill. They are simply pleasant interludes to relax our minds. They are fun in the same way that planning what we would do with lottery winnings is fun, but they aren't the sort of dreams that cause us to take action to make them a reality.

The dreams that drive this stage of our lives are the ones that could realistically be achieved and would truly bring satisfaction to our life. They might be big dreams, such as sailing around the world or writing a screenplay. They might be more modest, such as renovating your kitchen, learning to ride a horse, or reading the Mark Twain collection. They could even be as simple as finally getting around to organizing the books in your library. You undoubtedly can name several things you'd like to accomplish as a Resolutionist that fit all categories.

The trick to making these dreams a reality is to stop dreaming and start acting. Make a real commitment and stop viewing them as an "I wish I could" thing. Instead, turn them into an "I did that" thing.

MAKING A LIST, CHECKING IT TWICE OR MORE

Your dreams won't come true on their own. In fact, you might not even realize exactly what your dreams are. So the first thing to do is just brainstorm things you have always been interested in or wanted to try—dive the Great Barrier Reef, watch the entire Alfred Hitchcock collection of movies, perfect a beef bourguignon recipe, bungee jump in New Zealand. Be sure to include your passions in this list as well.

As an aside, you might be wondering what the difference is between a dream and a passion. In our minds a passion is the overriding drive that dreams are built on. It's a little like the difference between strategy and tactics. We have a passion for history. Our dream is to visit all US presidential libraries. Milledge has a passion for running. His dream is to run a marathon with ten different friends. Patti has a passion for her Chicago Cubs. Her dream is to see them play in every Major League ballpark. As you look at your passions, you can easily see how one might generate several dreams.

Now, as you begin to jot your dreams down, more ideas will surface than you can imagine. All of the interesting things that you have encountered or seen others experience. Resist self-censoring at this time. You might know that it is extremely unlikely that you will ever open a bakery, but if it is a dream, put it on the list.

MILLEDGE

Your dreams do not have to be "me-centered." One time at a family event, one of Patti's brothers mentioned that he would like to try foie gras. That was my cue to make his dream come true. I took him to one of my favorite French restaurants, and we spent a wonderful lunch with foie gras (turned out he *loved* it) and other French delicacies. It brought us both immense joy. Helping others turn their dreams into action is so rewarding at this stage, so I am continually on the lookout for those opportunities.

Once you have a good number of dreams, it's time to prioritize. The criteria for selecting the most urgent activities will be different for each individual. Perhaps you will prefer to focus first on those that require some level of physicality, which are better when you are young and nimble, or those that require long-distance travel or an extended time commitment to accomplish. You may also consider the expense associated with the experience—some are virtually free, while others require a significant investment. Are there activities on your list that you would like to share with others? Or some that will be a solo activity? Some can be spontaneous in nature, like buying a round of drinks for everyone in a bar, while others will take some planning, like completing our personal Tennis Grand Slam—Wimbledon, Australian Open, French Open, and US Open ("check"). Many dreams are a "one and done" experience like seeing the Northern Lights, and others are a pilgrimage like surfing the top fifteen beaches in the world. The screens that you use to organize your "dream board" will and should be personal. You may even choose to include a few that you can't control like "seeing the Chicago Cubs in the World Series" or "buying a winning lottery ticket." Dreams run the gamut, which is part of the excitement of converting them into life experiences.

We decided to make our dreams actionable by integrating them into our normal planning cycle by adding a few to our annual goal list but avoiding the rigidity that can threaten to turn dreams into chores. Each year we visit a new baseball park and a presidential library in our quest to see them all, and most of our travel plans consider some element of our "field of dreams." Tracking the great apes in Rwanda or whale watching in Alaska are included in our upcoming trips just as a carriage ride in Central Park and the thrill of the roller coaster at the Santa Cruz boardwalk were part of our past outings.

We have also used our dream adventures to connect with family and friends. Inviting others to share a caviar and champagne lunch or a visit to Mount Rushmore has added an element to realizing our dreams that was unexpected. The Rock & Roll Hall of Fame was far more interesting when shared with our brother (who knows every piece of rock music trivia), as was our visit to Green Bay's Lambeau Field when shared with good friends. Having a practical approach to taking a long list of dreams and turning them into realities that can be enjoyed by us as well as others has been exhilarating.

DREAMS DO NOT NEED TO BE HUGE

The dreams we put on our lists can be very basic. Some are individual dreams, while others involve both of us. One dream was to do a message in a bottle adventure. We each wrote a secret, personal message, put them in a bottle, and drove to the Pacific Ocean. We went to the edge of the water and tossed our message-filled bottles into the ocean. We hope that they are found and that one day our notes of inspiration touch a stranger. Another was to carve our initials into a tree to permanently commemorate our relationship. We chose a tree that we planted twenty years before and look forward to watching it grow for many years to come. These types of dreams are moments of joy. They bring back the childlike wonder in all of us.

We don't consider the size of the item or the effort involved when it comes to making the list. It's just as likely that a dream of swimming in the ocean at night will make the list as hiking the Camino de Santiago, a five-hundred-mile pilgrimage in Spain. Balancing small dreams, such as having a picnic on the beach at sunset, with elephant-size dreams, such as spending six months in a foreign country, lets you live life in technicolor rather than pastels.

PATTI

When we started our bucket list of dreams in 2008, we identified twenty-five items. Since then, we have completed forty-nine items, and the list has grown to sixty-five dreams, which include a few of the original twenty-five. It is amazing how easy it is to find things you want to try. As you change your lifestyle and begin meeting kindred spirits, you start seeing what they are doing and you add to your wish list. We might watch an interesting documentary about a topic or activity and say, "We should do that." Dreams are all around us if we just keep our eyes open.

While many are challenged by how big a dream is, don't let the size overwhelm you. Nearly all dreams can be broken down into smaller steps. Those smaller steps add up to a longer journey. We know one group of friends who met in college and have spent every Presidents' Day weekend visiting a different historical site. It has enabled them to stay in contact with each other, learn interesting events in history, and visit cities they never would have visited for any other reason. This is the type of dream that keeps on giving.

Sometimes the dream needs to be adjusted. In the earlier example, where we mentioned dreaming about opening a bakery, the dreamer might first consider selling cookies and cupcakes at a local farmers market. Or offering delicious cakes for special occasions to their loved ones. Taking steps toward a dream is still progress. One of us might want to swim like Michael Phelps. That's unlikely to happen, but we can still set a goal of swimming one hundred miles in a year. Sometimes we need to have dreams that likely won't be completely fulfilled but carry that slight "might happen" to make the future exciting and full of possibility.

WHEN DREAMS CRASH INTO REALITY

On occasion the best of dreams crash into the harsh world of reality. When prioritizing your dream list, be objective. Your dream may be to dance on the stage at the Kennedy Center. A more realistic dream would be to take ballroom dance lessons and enter yourself in a local dance competition. Take those lessons if you want to learn to dance, but be realistic about the outcome. Do it because you've always wanted to dance, not because you expect a standing ovation.

You might find that dreams do not always live up to your expectations. Tom and Linda always dreamed of retiring to a tropical island. Once they exited their very successful careers, they found the perfect home on the beach and settled in—sun, sand, waves; what is not to like? After the first twelve months, they both realized how much they missed the changing of the seasons, chilly nights around the fireplace, and the arrival of spring. Lucky for them, they had kept their family home in the Midwest and could divide their time between two places that they love. Dreams are just that … dreams. Once experienced, they may or may not be what we had hoped—but that is part of the adventure.

> Dreams are just that … dreams. Once experienced, they may or may not be what we had hoped—but that is part of the adventure.

MOVING FORWARD

Executing on your dreams is not always the endpoint. There are things on our current list that have been there since we began to catalogue our wishes. We may never get to them, but just imagining that we might gives us pleasure. However, none of your dreams will come true if you don't set up a process to move them from a dream list to an action list.

GIVE IT A TRY

- Sit down on a quiet afternoon and begin listing everything you have ever wanted to do or try.

- When you have the list, choose those you want to work on in the next year. Make it a mix of big and small.

- Choose one and get going!

LEVERAGE YOUR SUCCESS

*Only put off until tomorrow that which you are
willing to die having never done.*

—Pablo Picasso

WHEN WE WERE WORKING and needed to fill an open position, it was second nature to reach out to friends and colleagues who might be interested or might know someone. For example, Patti once filled a senior position at her company by calling a friend who had retired to Tuscany five years earlier. They had stayed in contact, and Patti knew her friend was growing bored in retirement and thinking about reentering the corporate world. It turned out to be a terrific match. They worked together for several years, leading to the sale of the company before both decided it was time for both of them to step back—this time for real.

Conversely, if we were ready for a new career challenge, we sought out those whom we thought could help or knew people who could help. If someone we knew asked for recommendations, we were always

> We don't need to give up connection-based interactions or the leverage they give us to reach our goals.

happy to be of assistance. Leveraging connections worked for everyone. It was how business got done.

As Resolutionists, we don't need to give up connection-based interactions or the leverage they give us to reach our goals. Admittedly, nurturing and using connections is not as easy as it was when we were working. While corporate networks just grew organically around us, there is no social network that allows us to find the perfect volunteer opportunity or learn that the local university has openings for adjunct faculty members. There is no easy way to let others know we are looking for a new member for our board or our tennis group. There is no LinkedIn for this stage of life. Instead, we have to rely on our own ingenuity, as well as a bit of luck.

For example, the chair of one of the largest nonprofit land trusts in California was originally asked to join the board of directors after his interest in environmental issues was expressed over a casual lunch. His career practicing law, along with his passion for protecting the public access to land in California, made him a perfect candidate, and the board was quick to welcome his engagement.

In order to make the best use of your relationships, communication is essential. The elevator pitch you've worked on in a previous chapter is perfect for this. You can even add something to your pitch to make your goals clearer and invite others to reach out. For example, "I'm currently serving on the board for the local Humane Society and have become involved with a group that uses horseback riding to help children with sensory issues. I have available time and would love to add a new cause, perhaps something in the performing arts."

When you begin talking to people and let them know what you might be interested in, you can be sure someone in the crowd will pick up the conversation and suggest a way to become involved. It will be up to you whether you follow up, but the connection will have been made.

By listening closely, you can also become the conduit between a person's interest and an appropriate activity. Maybe someone at a dinner party mentions that they enjoy cycling, and you offer to connect them with a group that cycles for charity. Maybe a friend mentions that they have joined a beer-brewing group, and you know someone who would also like to join. The idea is be aware of the connections you can take advantage of, as well as those you can facilitate.

PATTI

In an effort to leverage my success, I was searching for a mentoring opportunity. My preference was to contribute my knowledge and experience to the next generation by supporting an up-and-coming executive—ideally a young female leader. In a lunch conversation with a past business associate, I shared my desire, and as luck would have it, he had a situation in mind that he thought would be the perfect fit. A local arts organization had attracted a new leader to reenergize and reinvent an ages-old organization and art form. He made an introduction, and I knew in the first meeting that this was the perfect application of my skills and could not be a better use of my time. I am finding great joy in watching this young woman grow in her new role and being a part of the next generation of female leaders. And while I am making small contributions, I am realizing that I am "getting" much more than I am "giving," and if the arts community

> finds benefit in the improving health of this important
> pillar of their society—even better!

You don't need to wait for someone else to notice you would be a good fit or for you to randomly meet someone who would be perfect for a board position or volunteer role. This is where the networking skills you acquired come in handy. See something you are interested in? Reach out to someone who might help you secure an introduction. Conversely, be willing to be part of others' networks, and help make connections when asked.

Of course, you don't have to build a new network from scratch. Many of the people you interacted with during your career will still be in your orbit. Instead of connecting you with new employees or firms, however, they can connect you with organizations, activities, and people that will enhance your life as a Resolutionist. Both of us are active in organizations that now make up much of our after-career portfolio and were introduced to these opportunities by people we met through our previous associates.

MILLEDGE

A close friend from college and I stayed in touch as we built our careers in different parts of the country. One day she reached out to me asking for ideas about potential board members for a business in Virginia. I wanted to be helpful but was a little offended, having assumed that she didn't think I was the right person. She was asking for introductions, but I thought I already had a pretty good solution for the role—me.

Turns out she was trying to get me to say that I would be interested in it without pressuring me. She ultimately recruited me to join the board, and I have now served as chairman for the past six years. This board seat has been a terrific, interesting, educational, life-changing role for me, and I will be forever grateful. In fact, we partner each time we add new board members, as she has been the point person and instrumental in building a terrific board of directors. I know how much I appreciate the long-term relationship that we have.

REBALANCING YOUR PORTFOLIO

You might wonder why you need to nurture these social connections. The answer is simple: These connections will help you navigate your new world. Most of us spent the majority of our waking hours focused on our career and spent very little time in the world of philanthropy, arts, or anything else. That means we need to go on a bit of a journey to gather information about where our skills can be applied in a way that matters. We worked years to build a portfolio of networks, skills, and successes in the corporate world. Now we need to rebalance that portfolio so that it provides the outcomes that we want and need now.

When we worked, our portfolio of activities was likely allocated somewhere along the line of 60 percent career-related activities, 30 percent family-related activities, and 10 percent other activities, such as hobbies, continuing education, and philanthropy. It was really a rather straightforward life.

TIME SPENT ON ACTIVITIES DURING CAREER YEARS

HOBBIES
ADVENTURE
TRAVEL
LEARNING
HEALTH

FAMILY / FRIENDS

CAREER / WORK ACTIVITIES

Now that our career is behind us, it's time to reallocate our time. While our work life had just a few main steps on the pyramid, as Resolutionists our lives are much more varied. But filling in those extra layers isn't easy.

As much as we all liked to dream about what we'd do when we were no longer committed to a career, actually making that change can be harder than you think. For many of us, our time continues to revolve around industry-related activities. We continue to read industry publications. We meet with old work colleagues and talk about what they are doing. We continue to serve on industry-related boards. It's just so hard to step away. What helped us was ripping off the Band-Aid, as mentioned earlier.

When we moved to London, we had a chance to wipe the slate clean. After returning to the States, we can look at each opportunity that comes our way and make a decision based on whether it fits into our new portfolio. Do we really want to do it? Is it a positive addition to our life portfolio? Do our experience and interests align with the goals and needs of this cause?

Even with a clean slate, filling a portfolio is a bit of trial and error. It's very similar to balancing your investment portfolio. Even if you have your metrics and do your due diligence, on occasion you can still make a wrong decision.

We made some mistakes along the way by allowing ourselves to get pulled back into some of the things that we were ready to leave behind. We needed to purposefully step back and make sure we were engaging in things that brought us happiness and allowed us to make a difference. We needed to make sure we were leveraging our success and skills in our new life.

Over the years we have used a layering system to fill our new portfolios. We both have foundational commitments—sports and performing arts for Patti, poverty alleviation and corporate mentoring for Milledge—and then we have layered smaller or less time-consuming activities on top of those foundational passions. Whether large or small, however, we gravitate toward opportunities that allow us to apply our experience and knowledge to really have an impact. That is important. Before we embrace a new opportunity, we want to be certain that our time and resources really matter. And if they do, we are eager to pitch in!

The commitments in your portfolio will change as your interests and life change. You can often look ahead and know that there will come a time when a particular board position or philanthropic commitment will no longer be relevant. Maybe your skills are no longer needed. Maybe your work is complete, and it is time to let someone else take over. No matter what the reason, at some point there will be a hole in your portfolio that needs filling. Before that happens, begin to leverage your success to plant seeds and see what grows among your network. You might be pleasantly surprised.

TIME SPENT ON ACTIVITIES DURING POSTCAREER YEARS

ALONE TIME

HOBBIES

TRAVEL & ADVENTURE

HEALTH & FITNESS

FRIENDS | FAMILY | LEARNING

ORGANIZATIONAL COMMITMENTS

ENJOY YOUR SUCCESS

Leveraging your success runs along several separate tracks. One is using your old and new contacts to explore and become involved in new areas of interest. Another is to leverage your skills and knowledge to enhance the things that are now your focus. Still another is to use what you have earned and learned to enjoy this stage.

For example, we know a couple who spends a large portion of their time traveling. Some of the destinations are places they traveled to during their work life but didn't have time to get to explore. Others are places they've researched and dreamed of visiting. They aim to spend at least three months a year living in one of these countries. They might bicycle through France or rent a farmhouse in Devonshire. They will use these excursions as an excuse to gather their family for regular reunions that allow them to bond with grandchildren, nieces, and nephews in a way they couldn't when they were working, while introducing their family to diverse and engaging cultures. Closer to home, they have revisited places each of them has previously lived. Often they are surprised by what they learn now as adults that they missed as children or young adults living there.

Being able to indulge a love of travel comes partly from applying your financial resources, but you are also leveraging other things from your past success, such as your familiarity with the "ins and outs" of global travel. It takes a level of confidence to go to a foreign place where different languages are spoken and unfamiliar foods are served. Confidence comes with practice. The more you travel, the more comfortable it will be. We often travel with others, and we believe it adds an important dimension because we are seeing the world through their eyes as well as our own. You're leveraging the appetite that you built over your career for learning and experiencing things firsthand. Most people want to continue to learn, grow, and add new dimensions to themselves. Leveraging all of these factors of your success allows you to do that, as well as redefine your new portfolio for your new life.

MOVING FORWARD

Leveraging your success means more than using the wealth you've worked so hard for to make your current life fulfilled and joyful—though that is certainly a large part of it. It also means reaching out to contacts to access opportunities that would make your life more purposeful, as well as helping others access opportunities. And it means putting the things that made your work life so successful—confidence, wisdom, curiosity, problem-solving—to work. This is a time to leverage those skills for yourself and others.

GIVE IT A TRY

- Start by creating your own personal pyramids by using the examples in this chapter.

- Do an inventory of the tools that have resulted from your success.

- Design a plan to "leverage your success" to build a bridge from your past to your aspirational pyramid.

SURROUND YOURSELF WITH KINDRED SPIRITS

Kindred of spirit is all that matters.

—Bert McCoy

THIS IS THE PERFECT time in your life to surround yourself with those that share your perspective on how to live life. When we were gainfully employed, we were surrounded by people who shared our professional goals but not necessarily our personal goals. Now our focus is on building a social structure with people who challenge us, add color to our life, help us see the world differently, and encourage continual growth.

PATTI

When I was working, I was surrounded by kindred spirits, most of whom were supportive of my career. As I moved to the Resolutionist stage of life, I had to search harder to find supporters. They were not a natural part of my social fabric. After all, I had dedicated myself to my work. After I retired, most con-versations involved someone questioning my decision to retire. Many of their points were beginning to have an effect on me, and I was feeling as if I was letting down my generation of women. I had reached the top, and wasn't it my duty to help other women up the ladder? It became very difficult to say, "I know in my heart I'm ready to do this." So I had to really start finding myself in new places where I wasn't going to come away from a cocktail gathering, brunch, or coffee feeling like I was abandoning other women. I knew it was time for the next generation to step up, and I was ready to move on, but I needed to add a new support structure of individuals who would give me confidence about entering this new phase of my life. And that was going to require some effort on my part.

Whom would we consider a kindred spirit? For us, it means immersing ourselves in a group of people that embrace diversity in every way, including thoughts, opinions, and perspectives. It is *not* living in a bubble with others who agree on everything—but more a collection of individuals that capture the essence of *The Resolutionist*: engaged, informed, self-assured and full of adventure, always willing to take a risk to encourage others to think differently. We are on a common mission: to make the world and ourselves better by learning from each other and being challenged to understand differing points of view.

We've often heard the definition of an introvert to be someone who gains energy from solitude and that of an extrovert to be someone who gains energy through social interaction. Kindred spirits are people who gain energy from one another. Those that we consider kindred spirits exude "positive" energy that helps everyone in their orbit meet challenges and expand their horizons.

For example, we have a friend who has prioritized her work helping to lift young women out of poverty. She recently traveled to India with a group of similarly involved women. They enjoyed viewing historical sites and dining at interesting restaurants, as any traveler would. However, because they were all focused on a common mission, they also set up meetings with local officials to see how they were handling poverty in their region. These meetings, along with learning from her traveling companions, made it obvious that she could accomplish her objective with the limited resources she had available. She would not have scheduled the meetings or benefited from the knowledge exchange if she had not been traveling with a kindred group that was willing to include these meetings as part of its itinerary. Surrounding yourself with kindred spirits is not about encasing yourself in an echo chamber. It's about removing impediments to your growth and success.

FINDING FELLOW RESOLUTIONISTS

When we leave work, we lose about half of our social circle. And, unfortunately, it is often the half that we find to be the most stimulating and challenging. If we don't replace those interactions, we risk becoming socially

> Surrounding yourself with kindred spirits is not about encasing yourself in an echo chamber. It's about removing impediments to your growth and success.

isolated, which is harmful to your physical and mental health, no matter what your age.

According to researchers, social isolation carries the same level of health risks as obesity and smoking fifteen cigarettes a day.[11] In addition, those without a robust social circle

- Are at a higher risk of high blood pressure, coronary disease, and stroke

- Can experience a faster decrease in cognitive skills and greater likelihood of dementia because the mind is less active

- Have greater decline of functional skills, such as walking or climbing stairs

- Have a weakened immune system, possibly linked to stress

- Are at a higher risk of depression[12]

To combat that isolation, we need to nurture our social circles. Often people turn to their families and grandchildren to take the place of work colleagues. That is one option; after all, it is these very people that you missed during your career years. However, we all need peer relationships that are defined by a great sense of equality.

The key to having a healthier social life that includes your kindred individuals is knowing yourself. That would seem obvious, but it's not unusual for people to reach their postcareer life and realize they really don't know who they are. They've spent their life being told what to do and how to do it by parents, teachers, bosses, board members, and

11   Claire Pomeroy, "Loneliness is Harmful to Our Nation's Health," *Scientific American*, March 20, 2019, https://blogs.scientificamerican.com/observations/loneliness-is-harmful-to-our-nations-health/.

12   Amy Novotney, "The Risks of Social Isolation," *American Psychological Association Monitor* 50, no. 5 (May 2019), https://www.apa.org/monitor/2019/05/ce-corner-isolation.

others. Now you need to really look at what is important. What makes you feel secure and inspired? We found that the people that we are drawn to are curious, energetic, self-assured, and looking to expand their knowledge. They enjoy being challenged and love navigating a world where the answers aren't clear-cut.

PATTI

I grew up in a very blue-collar part of our country. It wasn't the "norm" to choose to further your education after high school. After all, there were an abundance of well-paid positions in the local factories—why would anyone secure a student loan and spend four more years in the education system when you could begin earning a respectable living now? My family and many of my friends questioned my decision to enroll in my university, and this pattern continued for many years of my life. Why was I moving to the East Coast and leaving my Midwestern roots? Why was I returning to work after my son was born? Why was I taking a promotion that would require my family to relocate? Why was I willing to travel for my job, leaving my son at home with a nanny? And eventually: Why would I choose to retire when the women's movement had so much progress still to be made? Defending every decision you make is exhausting and takes energy that can be better spent elsewhere. Finding strength from people who understand that my choices are mine and do not reflect on them allows me to focus my energies on growing and exploring rather than on defending. It

has been an important factor in making my postca·
reer life fulfilling and joyful.

Finding those with whom you share common values takes real effort. You can't just place an online ad looking for kindred spirits. It requires time, energy, and a willingness to experiment with new things. The more people that you come into contact with, the more likely you are to find those that enhance your life. If you are willing to embrace the notion of letting new and different people into your life, you will be much more approachable, and you will increase the likelihood that your kindred circle will grow and prosper. We have redefined our world by opening our arms and minds to any and every sort of person—you never know where the most profound human-interest stories will be. When we venture into the unknown of a social gathering filled with unfamiliar faces, we set out to meet a new person or two and to learn something brand-new over the course of the event. We find ourselves returning home with an expanded view of the human race.

Being open to new and changing relationships is a good start, but you also need to take proactive steps to make it happen. A few years ago, we took a house in Italy and invited another couple to accompany us. So far, the story is pretty standard. But to mix things up, we asked that couple to bring another couple that we didn't know, and we would bring along a couple that they didn't know. So we spent a week in Italy with two other couples that we knew, and one we did not. By the end, we were all the best of friends, and that friendship continues to this day. That really did not surprise us. The friends of our friends are very likely to be similarly interesting, engaging, and intellectually honest.

Philanthropy often connects people at this stage. We have the time, resources, and desire to give back. What we need is a supportive group that helps us find the best way to do that. When we moved back from London, we attended a few philanthropy-oriented workshops. We met several other couples that we now count as kindred spirits. They too were learning how to get better engaged in philanthropy.

But philanthropy is not the only way to meet people. Taking a class at a local community college, joining a theater group, volunteering, signing up to travel with a group, joining a tennis league, and any number of other activities can put you in contact with people who might become part of your social circle. You just have to make the effort.

THE SALON

Not too long ago, we were trying to find a way to deepen several of our relationships and to reinforce the scientifically supported need to be socially engaged. We wanted to make stronger and more meaningful bonds with those who were becoming an integral part of our lives. And we wanted to encourage the type of gatherings that provided the intellectual stimulation that we had enjoyed in our professional lives and were missing now. One of our ideas was to host an old-fashioned salon. We are in the early stages of forming our salon but are finding great camaraderie in the discussions and debates.

A salon is a gathering of people who come together under one roof to amuse one another and to increase their knowledge through conversation. Salons can be traced back to the courtyards of sixteenth-century Italy, but they are better known for flourishing over the next two centuries in France. They continued among the educated elite through the years and saw something of a heyday among intellectuals in the 1920s. Gertrude Stein and Alice B. Toklas hosted one of the more celebrated salons of the time—maybe of all time. Their Saturday evening salons (in their literal French salon) included artists and intellectuals, such as Picasso, Matisse, Hemingway, Sinclair Lewis, Thornton Wilder, and scores of other great thinkers, writers, and artists of the day. Their salon became so synonymous with salons that Ernest Hemingway mentioned them in one of his novels, and Woody Allen featured them in his movie *Midnight in Paris*.

Our salon doesn't quite reach the intellectual level of the Stein-Toklas salon, but it has become a much-anticipated fixture in our lives. In building our salon, we were purposeful in our construction—seeking out those that have the Resolutionist characteristics: full-time work in the past and an unending level of curiosity. The salon will only be as successful as the participants allow. It requires a willingness to listen, contribute, debate, and discuss in an open and productive fashion. The salon as a body exists to educate its members as individuals through the experiences of the entire group.

For us, having a broad universe of engaged "saloners" works. But there is no "best" size. Salons can be small, with just six or eight people, or they can be large, with fifty or more. The only requirement is that members of the group be compatible in their desire to learn from others, be respectful of differing opinions, and make a meaningful contribution to the group. It's about fulfilling the need to grow, learn, exchange ideas, and have social interaction.

To simplify the logistics, we host at the same place and the same time. However, we rotate leaders among the group. Each leader is responsible for choosing that session's topic. Although salons have the reputation for being highbrow, they don't have to be. The topics can be high level and philosophical or very basic. They can include things such as voter registration, social media, antiracism, a new app or technology, a favorite book or movie—literally anything that will generate conversation and a variety of viewpoints. We debated a very important element of our salon and decided that we did not want the topic to drive participation, so we do not disclose the subject matter in advance. When people don't know the topic, they come feeling like they're on a bit of a journey or treasure hunt. They might find out it's a topic they normally would not have thought to discuss, but they enjoy the fact that they learn something new. We assume that everyone has something to contribute to every topic, and in fact, those with the least amount of knowledge often move the conversation along because they look at it with fresh eyes. They'll ask the questions and express reactions that others with more detailed knowledge might not think to ask. It is so much more interesting to have a variety of opinions and knowledge levels than to talk about something everyone has studied in depth.

The salon has proven to be an efficient framework for bringing people together in a way that encourages growth. We leave each one energized and eager for the next one. But it has also proven to be a good way to make a kindred connection, as everyone is encouraged to suggest other potential members. It's become an evergreen method of learning, living, and laughing with other Resolutionists. We would certainly call this outcome the epitome of leveraging success.

MOVING FORWARD

Seeking kindred spirits does not mean that you are looking for duplicates of yourself. Nor does it mean that everyone exhibits the Resolutionist qualities in the same way. Although we want the people surrounding us to be curious and adventurous, some will be more likely to exhibit those qualities while sharing our passion for making a difference, while others might prefer to indulge in philosophical discussions. Some will be perfect travel companions, while others are the foundation of a must-attend book club. Like the Venn diagrams in the previous chapter, there will be overlap, but they won't be identical. And how boring would it be if everyone were identical? That's not the Resolutionist way.

GIVE IT A TRY

Hosting a salon has worked so well for us that we've included a cheat sheet that might help you launch your own. Give it a try!

BEST PRACTICES FOR HOSTING A SALON

<u>Definition of a salon:</u> A gathering of people under one roof held partly to amuse one another and partly to refine the taste and increase the knowledge of participants through conversation.

<u>Things that remain constant:</u>

- Location: same location every time

- Day/Time: same day/time to simplify

<u>Things that change:</u>

- Host

- Topic

- Refreshments and snacks

<u>Other:</u>

- Do not disclose the topic in advance. Instead, "go on a journey" together.

- Sample topics: Although salons are geared to intellectual discussions and have the reputation of being philosophical in nature, the topics can be quite diverse—wine, food, best beaches, best technology, green energy, time management hacks, is bowling a sport, and so on.

- Refreshments and snacks: Keep it simple and easy.

- Administrator: Even though the host changes, keep one person as the administrator to manage RSVPs, communication, and so on.

SAMPLE INVITATION:

Dear Friends,

As a part of our continuing quest for learning, growing, and laughing, we would like to sponsor the creation of a Silicon Valley Salon in 2020. The salon comes from seventeenth-century France and is "a gathering of people under one roof of an inspiring host, held partly to amuse one another and partly to refine the taste and increase the knowledge of participants through conversation." The concept is to gather on a regular basis to share something that you have found to be useful, enjoyable, profound, or new at this stage of putting a finer point on your life. This can be an investment idea, a wine, an app, a gadget, a restaurant, a movie, a book ... or anything that strikes you!

Our cadence for gathering will be bimonthly in 2020, always from 4:30 p.m. to 6:30 p.m. on Thursdays: February 20, April 9, June 25, August 27, October 22, and December 17.

We have selected you because we think that you will make the salon more engaging, interesting, and informative. We encourage attendance as couples or individuals, as your life allows. The guidelines for the group are:

- Each session will be hosted by one of the members.

- The host is required to cover the costs and be responsible for the experience.

- You are encouraged to add people that you think might be interested and interesting.

- We agree to administer the group, sending emails and managing RSVPs and calendar as necessary.

- We will host our first gathering on February 20, so please RSVP to the first event, and we will inform you of the location once we have a better sense of head count.

We hope that you will find the addition of the salon to be a positive way to learn and grow with others and, maybe, make a new friend along the way!

Please mark your calendars and RSVP to the inaugural event!

DEVELOP A NEW METRIC SYSTEM

When you measure what you are speaking about, and
express it in numbers, you know something about it.

—Lord Kelvin

WE ALL LIKE to think that we are self-motivated and would reach for the stars, whether anyone recognized our achievements or not. Surprisingly, that is not how humans work. Having our success recognized is one way we build more confidence, remain relevant, and feel self-assured enough to take on additional challenges. We need outside validation to keep going.

For most of our lives, this outside validation was easy to come by. We had parents, teachers, coaches, and bosses who set goals and let us know when we succeeded, as well as when we failed. Knowing that you are progressing is crucial to staying motivated.

The authors of *The Four Disciplines of Execution*[13] give an example of how being able to see how well you are doing is an important factor

---

13   Chris McChesney, Jim Huling, and Sean Covey, *The Four Disciplines of Execution*, 2012, https://www.amazon.com/Disciplines-Execution-Achieving-Wildly-Important-ebook/.

in keeping your eye on your goal. In their story a high school football team decided to play despite the damage Hurricane Katrina had done to their stadium. Much of the infrastructure, including the scoreboard, had been destroyed, but the field was still playable. The game was lack. This was a top-ranked team with enthusiastic fans, but without the scoreboard, the fans found their attention drifting. Instead of watching the game, they were talking among themselves. There wasn't nearly as much cheering or enthusiasm. And without the cheering from the bleachers—and a constant reminder of the score and time left in the game—the players were sluggish. Their play lacked emotion. The team needed the roar of the crowd, and the crowd needed the scoreboard, to stay focused and engaged in the game.

We all need some type of scoreboard to make sure we are hitting the mark, whether that mark involves athletic, corporate, financial, or personal goals.

However, without the natural validation that comes from a business environment, you would need to create an infrastructure that provides you the acknowledgment that you thrive on. How do you set up a new metric to let you know that life is still purposeful and you are reaching your goals?

The same way you would set up any metric system: You define the end goal, you determine what is necessary to reach that goal, and then you determine appropriate metrics to track your progress. Let's see how that might work now that we are not dealing with sales quotas and stock prices.

CHANGING THE DEFINITION

It's impossible to measure success if you haven't defined what success looks like. What is your desired outcome? How will you know when you're making progress? During our working days, success often meant winning. And winning meant someone else lost. You beat the competition to market. You were promoted over someone else. You convinced the team to do things your way. You were recognized as top employee or landed a spot on a top ten list. But now, in this stage of life, we don't think about winning in the same way. Winning is no longer defined strictly by competitiveness or someone else losing. It's more personal. It's accomplishing goals and winning for yourself as opposed to only knocking out the competition.

PATTI

When we lived in London, I would go for a walk in Hyde Park every day. I would start out walking with Milledge, but then he would split off to go for a run. This had been our routine for about two weeks when I thought, *Wow. I've been walking every day in the park for fourteen days. That's such an accomplishment.* But then I thought, what was I really measuring? And why was I measuring it? I began to think more about my walks. Was it really an accomplishment to walk fourteen days in a row? And even if it was, did it matter? If it doesn't matter, why am I doing it? And if it does matter, is the number of days walked the correct way to capture what matters? This was the moment that I realized that I still needed metrics in my life, but they were going to be very different than those I had used previously. I decided to *stop* measuring the consecutive walks and began to measure the activities within the walk—new people I said "good morning" to, how my favorite tree changed over the seasons, which new flowers were in bloom, the growth of the baby ducks on the lake—and I began to drop into the art gallery in the middle of the park to see the latest exhibition. I realized that it was never really about the walk but the experiences that my time in the outdoors afforded me.

Success now is more tightly intertwined with collaboration, such as helping a nonprofit or board be more successful. Or it's achieving an intangible goal, such as increasing happiness. It's not a zero-sum game anymore.

Because we are redefining success and winning to be more personal, we need to change what our scoreboard looks like.

Many of the goals for Resolutionists can still be measured by looking at actual results. We can track how many countries we've visited or how many new recipes we've tried. We regularly review our financial progress and our spending against our annual budget. We can look at our virtual whiteboard and note how many of our annual goals have been met.

But how do you measure happiness? How do you measure personal health? How do you measure contentment or the strength of your relationship? We've never viewed our relationships with each other and with friends and family—the connective tissue we had to the universe—as measurable. Yet those connections are crucial to remaining healthy and relevant in "retirement." How do we know we are keeping them strong?

MEASURING THE UNMEASURABLE

After a lot of false starts, we realized that we could break down an intangible, such as happiness, into discrete parts, which could be tracked and measured. If we wanted to *increase* happiness, we needed to look at the things in our life that *contribute to our* happiness. If we accomplished the parts, then by inference we were achieving the whole. So we gave ourselves a challenge: Name the unmeasurable goals we wanted to experience or accomplish; then define the various parts and look at how well we were achieving them.

PATTI

During my first year of "retirement," I decided to become reacquainted with my jewelry collection by wearing a different piece of jewelry each day. Even if some pieces had lived in the back of a drawer for the past several years, it was time to bring them back into my life. I had acquired each of them for a reason. At one time I thought each piece was beautiful and that it would make me happy. And so, every day, no matter what we were doing, I would wear a different piece of my jewelry, and it brought me a newfound happiness. It reminded me where and why I got it, and what the story around it was. Maybe it was a piece that came from my grandmother, or maybe it was a piece that Milledge had given me for a special thing, or it was something bought on a vacation. I couldn't measure happiness, but I could set a goal of wearing a different piece of jewelry and make sure I achieved that goal, which in turn increased my level of happiness.

Let's start with happiness. The first step in this process would be to look back over the past year and ask yourself, "What made me happy or brought me joy during this time?" Was it people? Was it material things? Was it experiences? Was it learning? Once you have a list of things that you derive happiness from, you can begin to zero in on how you can do more of those things.

For example, we know that spending quality time with good friends makes us happy. We can't measure happiness per se, but we can measure how much time we spend with friends. Thus our hypothesis becomes: If doing interesting things with friends brings happiness, then meeting with friends more often will bring increased happiness. To test that hypothesis, we purposefully schedule time to share experiences and create memories with friends. The amount of time can be measured and act as a proxy measurement for happiness.

In the same way, if you are focused on reducing stress in your life, then identify those things that can eliminate some of that tension. We had no idea how to measure stress levels—with the exception of checking our blood pressure. So we looked for obvious activities that would bring more calm into our daily lives. We added twenty minutes each day of meditation to reflect on the previous day and to prepare for what activities were slated for the next twenty-four hours. We added music to our daily routine to fill some of the moments, such as those spent doing mundane chores and tasks or cooking a meal, when doubt and anxiety can creep into your mind. Patti dedicated herself to more laps in the pool for her "think time," and we both limited our consumption of network news to the bare minimum. We could see how making these slight adjustments to our life allowed us to live a less frenetic life and to benefit from a decrease in overall stress.

In both of these examples, we are not measuring the end goal. We are looking at the things that are components of the bigger picture.

MILLEDGE

Every year for as long as I can remember, I would create an annual goal list. When Patti and I married, we morphed it into a joint list that included family goals along with individual goals. Over the years, the main goal categories (finance, business, health, resolution, renunciation, and a to-try list) evolved, but not dramatically. I like order and structure, and knowing my priorities for the coming year gave me a sense of purpose. In addition, if it went on the list, I would get it done. However, a couple of years after Patti and I stopped full-time work, putting together the list became much more challenging. Frankly, there were at least twenty things that we wanted to do during the next year or so, but they didn't fit the categories. This was an "ah-ha" moment when it really hit me that postcareer goals and ambitions were very different from those in my previous life. The categories didn't work anymore. We needed to adapt our system to our new life, rather than trying to fit our new goals into the old system. It has taken us some time to determine the proper categories, but once we dialed it in, the goal list continued to be an incredibly useful tool to live our best lives. It also taught us a very valuable lesson—the goal list, like most things in life, needed to evolve as our lives evolved.

Looking at multiple dimensions of a goal can provide you with many ways to measure the "unmeasurable." Once we began to purposefully look at the factors that create a state of happiness, we realized that it isn't just people. Other things in our life also bring happiness. We looked at how those could be measured. For example, both of us like to keep things simple. We don't like waste. We don't like to have stuff just for the sake of having stuff. So we decided that simplifying our lives would make us happier. But "simplify" is another one of those intangibles that is hard to measure. How would we define simple? How would we know when we'd reached our goal?

As we often do, we started with a list. We brainstormed everything we could eliminate, consolidate, or change to make our life easier. As we checked things off this list, we were motivated to keep going.

MILLEDGE

When possible, we always look to layer multiple types of "happiness promoters" on top of each other to leverage their effect. For example, Patti loves hot tea. She especially loves to have a cup of tea every morning before she gets out of bed. For most of her life, she only drank Lipton English Breakfast tea. But she has challenged herself to try other flavors, and the surprise at finding those she likes brings her joy. For my part, I love bringing tea to her every morning. It makes me happy to be able to do something so simple yet so meaningful on several different levels. For us, that simple cup of hot tea signifies love and the happiness we find in each other.

Some of the things that might be on such a list would include doing a spring cleaning to reduce the clutter in your home, unsubscribing to duplicate or unused subscriptions, and consolidating investment accounts (it's not unusual to have several 401(k) accounts because you've changed employers and didn't move the retirement account). One of the things we did was challenge ourselves to wear everything in our closet in a year. Anything not worn would be considered "wasteful" and donated to an organization that needed it since we obviously didn't. This challenge resulted in Milledge putting on a tuxedo to go out to dinner one night because it was the one thing in his closet he hadn't had a chance to wear, and he knew he would need it again someday. But it also showed us just how much stuff we had accumulated that we really didn't need. Donating our unneeded clothes to an organization that could use them brought us satisfaction on two fronts. Having fewer "things" made us feel lighter and happier. But we also felt good about helping others.

MERGING OLD WITH NEW

We've been talking about developing new metrics because the things that are important to us now are largely intangible. But that's not true about everything. Our life is still full of things that can be measured in the usual way. We use the same metrics we always have to judge our wealth management and health and fitness progress. We find validation in being invited to speak at an event, being asked to teach a class at the local university, or being recruited to serve on a board. All prove that we are still viewed as intelligent, relevant people with something to offer. When we see nonprofits that we are involved with make progress or receive awards, we get personal validation.

So we aren't throwing out the old. We are just adding new layers that allow us to measure the types of things that are important to us now. This new system will have new categories, such as happiness, adventure, learning, relationships, and the like, that weren't discrete goals in our previous life. We certainly wanted to be happy and have strong relationships, but they weren't goals to be measured. To some degree, we just hoped that they would happen.

THE ROLE OF DEADLINES

Our life has been full of deadlines. Someone needed an answer by the end of the day. Projects needed to be done by the end of the month. Quarterly results needed to be posted. Annual budgets needed to be submitted. We have lived our life in three-month, six-month, or annual increments, and getting a project done within a specific time period was always part of your success. The turn of the clock from December 31 to January 1 was monumental. You felt like you were wiping the slate clean and starting fresh each year.

It's not like that anymore. The start of a new year is just that—a one-page turn of the calendar. We have now reached a time of life when we can take our foot off the gas. You are no longer ruled by a calendar structure. There might be a few things that still need to be done on a short-term deadline—raising money for a nonprofit that needs a specific amount of capital to fund its projects comes to mind—but many more of the goals at this stage are fluid. You are marching toward accomplishing them without a clock ticking. The pressure is off. And this can be both a blessing and a challenge. Without a deadline, it can be hard to stay motivated. That means you need to redefine what "deadline" means when planning your goals. You don't want the pressure of corporate deadlines, but having a limited time frame helps you do the things that need to be done to reach your goal.

We have mentioned before that we have a whiteboard with annual goals—the things we want to do within a year. These are, of course, soft deadlines. It's not the end of the world if we only get to two ballparks this year rather than the three we want to, or if we only see one new presidential library instead of the three we had our hearts set on. But having an end date is important to keep your focus. Without that deadline, it is too easy to procrastinate.

We also have long-term goals with hard-stop deadlines, such as visiting one hundred countries before we die (at least we hope that is long-term). Many of our friends have this same type of overarching goal with an unknown but undeniable deadline, such as scuba diving at the top twenty scuba sites or completing the Seven Summits Challenge before they are physically unable to do so. To reach these long-term goals, we have several shorter-term deadlines that include reaching a specific training level by a certain date or saving enough to pay for each leg of the challenge by the end of the year. If you can set some longer-term goals for yourself that influence the way you live your life between now and when you accomplish it, that's the pinnacle. That's when you're really thinking about living your life.

Unlike our work deadlines, however, these deadlines are self-imposed. They are more mental than actual. This is a good thing. Although not having firm deadlines means you have to find internal motivators, having a life where goals are evergreen and intertwined with your lifestyle is much more fulfilling than completing a report, filing it away, and moving on to another discrete project.

MOVING FORWARD

Adjusting your definition of success and the metrics that you will use to know when you have won will make your life purposeful and fulfilling. We wish we had done that when we first left our careers. It would have made the transition to becoming a Resolutionist much easier.

GIVE IT A TRY

- If you are currently using a metric system, check to ensure that it reflects this phase of your life and that you have mastered the art of measuring the unmeasurable.

- If you aren't currently using a metric system, choose four metrics, both measurable and unmeasurable, that are important to you.

- Design a system and a cadence to monitor progress.

- Don't be afraid to make your metric system evergreen. Things do change!

SAY GOODBYE TO FOMO

All we have to decide is what to do with the time that is given us.

—JRR Tolkien

ONE OF OUR FIRST steps in writing this book was to solicit input from friends and acquaintances to better understand their experiences as they exited the  workforce and to learn from what they did or didn't do in preparation. What would they have done differently? We heard many different answers, but one really made us stop and think about how we were living our lives.

"I wish I had the courage to prioritize activities that were for my benefit. I could have allowed myself to be more selfish. I felt obligated to represent my company, employees, investors, and customers to the greatest extent possible, which resulted in a schedule that was full of appointments that caused me to be at the center of my professional universe. But I didn't tend to my own needs. I didn't get the message that is repeated on every flight: 'Put your oxygen mask on first before you help others.'"

This discomfort associated with putting yourself first carries over into the early part of "retirement."

The fear of missing out (FOMO) affects everyone from childhood to old age. And making choices based on assumptions, expectations, and judgments doesn't lead to the sort of life that you deserve.

Researchers at McGill University and Carleton University conducted a study that looked at how FOMO affected college students. Turns out it affected nearly every aspect of their day. No matter what they were doing, there was always something going on elsewhere that they thought they were missing out on. This was particularly true if they were doing a required task such as studying or working. But even if they were hanging with a group of friends or attending a party, they often thought another group or party might be having more fun. It caused stress and often caused them to make less than optimal decisions. In addition, FOMO was associated with increasing negative emotions, fatigue, physical symptoms, and decreased sleep.[14]

FOMO is tied to insecurity, which is more obvious in students and younger adults. But that doesn't mean that those achieving Resolutionist status are immune. Starting a new and completely different phase of life will make anyone insecure. When we were working, we often attended a conference or hosted a work dinner to meet people or further our career. Now we are looking to fill our time and use our talents in brand-new ways, and we often aren't quite sure what those ways are. So what happens? We say yes because we are afraid of missing out on a great opportunity.

---

14   Milyavskaya, M., Saffran, M., Hope, N., et al. "Fear of Missing Out: Prevalence, Dynamics, and Consequences of Experiencing FOMO," *Motivation and Emotion* 42 (2018), 725–737, https://doi.org/10.1007/s11031-018-9683-5.

Your calendar can look pretty empty when you stop full-time work. You wonder if anyone even remembers you. Everything looks interesting because you long for the frenetic lifestyle that you left behind. As we mentioned in an earlier chapter, we all look for validation that we are still relevant. It's a relief to know that someone is interested in what we have to offer. Besides, nearly all of us like helping other people. If someone says they need us, we don't want to disappoint. But every opportunity is not the right opportunity. Our challenge in this stage is to develop a set of guidelines that help us sort through all the possibilities and find the ones that matter.

> **If someone says they need us, we don't want to disappoint.**

DEVELOP A DECISION TREE

With all of the opportunities that you will find coming your way, having a logical and consistent way to decide which ones to accept will make your decisions more obvious. We have found that a newly designed decision tree has worked for us. You will, of course, have a list of things that are important to you, but an example of what we look at includes:

SHOULD I ENTERTAIN THIS REQUEST?

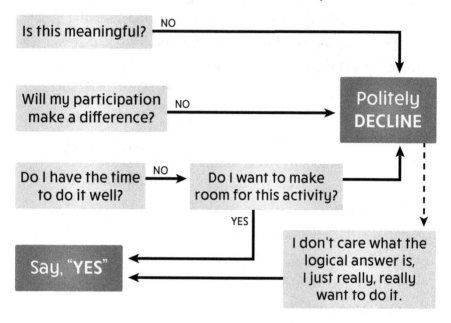

IS THIS OPPORTUNITY MEANINGFUL?

If yes, then give it a closer look. If no, why are we even thinking about it?

There is no reason at this stage to do things for any other reason than you choose to. In the past we often did things because of the perceived negative consequences of not doing them. We attended numerous trade shows, conferences, dinners, and meetings because of what might possibly happen if we weren't there, as well as any benefit we might derive from it. You now have the luxury of leaving half of the equation behind. Accentuate the positive. Embrace an opportunity because of the positive benefits it brings to your life instead of simply attempting to avoid the negative.

PATTI

A year or so after my final company was sold, I was invited to an industry luncheon that had become something of a tradition in the last ten years of my professional career. It was viewed as a "must-do" event—so I agreed to go. When the day arrived, I looked at it on my calendar and thought, *I don't know why I am dedicating three hours to this activity, but I always go.* So off I went.

When I arrived, I looked at the other attendees, and thought, *These good people are not a part of my current life.* But I went ahead and sat down with the old gang. As is customary, everyone began gossiping about the industry. Who was in—who was out. What products were going to win the day at the trade show. The normal speculation and innuendo that goes with industry events. After about thirty minutes and the salad course, I looked outside and saw it was a beautiful day. I thought, *If I leave now, I can get home, change my clothes, and enjoy a nice long walk before dark.* I thought, *This could not be less interesting or relevant to my life today*, and so I took the opportunity to escape.

As I was walking and enjoying the outdoors, I reminded myself that I had to get over the fear of missing something and, instead, be driven to do something because it's additive to my life. That day was the big switch for me. I realized that I was not missing out on anything by leaving the old industry events to the next generation. In fact, holding onto the past meant that I was actually missing out on something that brought me happiness now.

WILL MY PARTICIPATION MAKE A DIFFERENCE?

If yes, continue to consider the request. If not, politely decline.

No matter how much free time you have, it is still a limited resource. And in fact, it is your most precious asset and is fully within your control. Treat it responsibly. Applying your time to a situation where your experience, skills, advice, and counsel can move things forward is important to your well-being and sense of self. You're not just trying to fill your time. You're investing your time, and like in all good investments, you strive for positive returns.

MILLEDGE

As chairman of an investment bank, I am presented with a number of potential deal opportunities. About a year ago, my firm was making a presentation and I had to jump through hoops to fly halfway across the country because one of the VCs thought it was critically important that I was there. He insisted there was no deal without me. We did the presentation, and we lost the deal. I was so relieved. For the first time in my life, I wasn't disappointed over the loss. All I could think was, *This deal is not worth the commitment of time, energy, and effort to work with people that I'm not inspired by.* For me, that was a real lesson that I was in a different place than I'd ever been.

DO I HAVE THE TIME TO DO IT WELL?

If yes, entertain the request. If no, is the opportunity compelling enough to reprioritize your other activities?

An opportunity might have all the characteristics that make it the perfect fit. But if you don't have adequate time to do it well, this isn't the time to say yes. Stretching yourself too thin helps no one. You will disappoint yourself and others. If, however, you'd really like to try to make it work, look at the other things you are doing. Is there something you can ease out of? Our commitments ebb and flow. Something that was really interesting a year ago might not be so now. Maybe we've provided all the help we can, and it's now up to someone else to take it to the next level. Maybe it turned out that it wasn't quite the right fit after all. Sometimes we don't realize that it is time to leave something that is no longer fulfilling until we have an alternative staring us in the face.

DO I WANT TO SAY YES NO MATTER WHAT LOGIC SAYS?

Sometimes we just have to do what we have to do. We don't have the time. But something is calling us. In that case, dive in. You will probably be stretching yourself thin, but assume it will be a short-term situation. It might take the place of activities that are less attractive when compared to your new venture, and you will drop the old to make room for the new. Or not. It might very well turn out that the new opportunity is the one to drop, just as your decision tree predicted.

But life would be very dull if every aspect were governed by lists and decision trees. Use logic to help you keep your life in control and to focus your energy on the right things—but every now and then, take a chance. Taking a flyer can feel so good!

REFRAMING THE QUESTION

When it comes to resisting the temptation of making decisions based on FOMO, it helps to reframe why we are doing things. We view our activities as part of a life portfolio. Just as with our investment strategy, each asset in a life portfolio will have a reason for being there. When we worked, our time was heavily weighted toward career activities. Now we have the luxury of being more fluid.

During our career days, if you could squeeze a new project into the day, you would take it on. You might fear missing out on a better project if you rejected this one. The only question we asked was: Can I physically fit it into my day? If yes, then it passed the test.

Now we don't ask ourselves if we *can* fit something into our portfolio. We ask ourselves if we *want* to fit it in. Does it add meaning? Does it fit our new metric system? Now we think about our capacity differently because we aren't looking to fill each slot in the calendar. We are simply looking to engage in activities that bring us fulfillment. We allocate our time differently. To continuing education or to health and wellness or to our relationships with family and friends. All of those things are scheduled in the same way a business meeting would have been added to our calendar in the past. Sometimes we will say we don't have time for something, but that really means that particular opportunity isn't a priority in our life portfolio. Because our new way of looking at time commitments provides a fluidity we've never had before, we can almost always find the time if it is something that we expect to enjoy.

This fluidity means we can choose to spend significantly more time on some things than others just because we feel they are important. For example, COVID-19 has impacted several of the organizations we support. Being able to devote a significant amount of our time to providing guidance on how to best handle the challenge is energizing. It gives us purpose. Unlike the story Patti tells, where a one-hour phone call felt like a lifetime, we are happy to devote hours and hours to help these organizations survive.

PATTI

Guarding your time and being aware of decisions based on FOMO is an ongoing process. It's been a few years since I left my last full-time career assignment, but not long ago I allowed myself to engage in a situation because I was flattered that someone needed me, that someone thought I was worthwhile, that someone found me impressive. This person asked me if I was willing to do some consulting work around an industry's reaction to COVID-19, and I was excited to do it. We had our first call, which was supposed to be the beginning of a series of calls over the next few weeks. The gentleman could not have been more pleasant and delighted with the conversation. After I hung up, I thought, *I just feel like I had the life sucked out of me.* It was an excruciating hour of looking backward. Afterward I reached out to him to let him know it wasn't the right fit and I wasn't interested in continuing the work. Five years ago I would have jumped at the chance to share my experience and wisdom about the industry's response to COVID-19 and which companies would emerge the strongest. But I'm in a different place now. Milledge tried to warn me that this wasn't right, but there was nothing he could do or say to convince me this wasn't going to be wonderful. I had to find out for myself, which I did. Sometimes we need this type of reminder that our focus is different now and life is better because of it.

It's also important to mention that you can change your mind. For so many of us, once we've committed to something, we feel we have to see it through to the end. But that is not the case. The end is when you decide it no longer fulfills a need for you. As Patti illustrates in her stories, if something isn't working, it's OK to politely change course. Get up and leave the lunch before it is too late. Call the client back and explain that the relationship isn't working. Don't let a false sense of duty or FOMO keep you in a situation that no longer satisfies you (or maybe never did).

Although you now have an abundance of time, the longer you live, the more value your time has because it is an expiring asset. The older you get, the less time will be available. Spend every single hour of those limited years doing something that lifts you up.

Our rational mind understands this time limitation well, but we really need to embrace it emotionally. What *you* want is important. Don't let others guilt you into saying yes when you should say no. People will fight over an inch of land, they will go to the ends of the earth to get repayment on a small debt, but they will let someone consume hundreds of hours of their time. If you have a clear vision of what really matters, you will be able to resist the pull of FOMO.

One final observation. Being judicious with how you spend your time doesn't mean you never take a chance on an opportunity that falls outside your comfort zone. It helps to have some general guidelines when it comes to evaluating options, as we illustrated in the decision tree, but those are just a framework. Sometimes you need to step outside the framework to add spice to your life. It is similar to adding a risky alternative investment to your portfolio. It might not pan out, but if it does, it will add a boost to your returns that you wouldn't have had otherwise. And if the new opportunity doesn't work? Well, you step back, dust yourself off, and focus on the things that *are* working.

MOVING FORWARD

You have wisdom, resources, a network, and now the most precious asset of all—time. You will get more requests to participate in a variety of activities than you ever imagined. They will all sound wonderful. But if you are not careful, you can find yourself running from one shiny object to another and never truly feeling that you are satisfying your own needs. If you have been following the resolutions in this book, you have found your own passions and goals, as well as new ways to define success. The next step is to overcome your history of associating activity with relevance. Learn to value unscheduled time and align your actions with your new mission.

GIVE IT A TRY

- Review your activities for the past six months.

- Highlight those that you found to be fulfilling and productive and those that you engaged in simply because you were afraid of missing out.

- Look for the common thread among these activities.

- Resolve to double-check yourself when you commit to something, large or small.

- Do a regular review of your time allocation to align with your Resolutionist life.

CONCLUSION

CREATING A NEW MODEL FOR GENERATIONS THAT FOLLOW

Some guy said to me, "Don't you think you're too old to sing rock 'n' roll?" I said: "You'd better check with Mick Jagger."

—Cher

AS WE WRITE THIS BOOK, it is 2020 and we are several months into the shelter-at-home orders put in place to fight the COVID-19 pandemic. People are getting bored and antsy. They've cleaned their houses until they sparkle. They've planted gardens and made long-needed home repairs. They've read every book on the bookshelf or tablet and, perhaps, organized said bookshelf by size and color. They've attended Zoom wine parties, continuing education classes, family reunions, baby showers, weddings, and funerals. Now they are done. If they ever see another one-thousand-piece jigsaw puzzle, it will be too soon. They want to get back to their lives. It's not unusual to hear people say something like, "If this is what retirement is like, I'm never going to stop working!"

And, frankly, the past few months have been very similar to what most people envision when they think about "retirement." After all, isn't that what we've grown up seeing in the generations before us? Once someone stops working, they just seem to fade into the background. It's as if becoming a retiree suddenly turns energetic, active, curious people into shadows of their former selves.

In fact, that's exactly what often happens. Researchers have found that there is something called the "stereotype threat," which means that when people are presented with stereotypes of their group—retirees, women, scientists, athletes, and so on—they tend to unconsciously take on those stereotypical characteristics. So if older folks are told they are irrelevant, tired, and less quick-witted after they leave their career lives, they tend to begin acting in ways that confirm that stereotype. The most widely cited study illustrating this phenomenon[15] divided a contingent of older adults into three groups. One group read a series of articles linking age to cognitive decline. Another read articles that described the contributions to society being made by people over the age of sixty-five, including scientists, politicians, businesspeople, and others. The third group did no reading. All three groups were then asked to remember a sequence of random words. It would be reasonable to expect that all of the groups would remember about the same number of words. After all, there were no physical or cognitive differences among the groups. In fact, the group that had been reading about declining cognitive health was able to recall significantly fewer words than either of the other two groups. They had been reading

---

15   Thomas Hess, Corinne Auman, Stanley Colcombe, and Tamara Rahhal, "The Impact of Stereotype Threat on Age Differences in Memory Performance," *The Journals of Gerontology* Series B: Psychological Sciences and Social Sciences 58 (2003), 3–11, doi:10.1093/geronb/58.1.P3. https://www.researchgate.net/publication/6146808_The_Impact_of_Stereotype_Threat_on_Age_Differences_in_Memory_Performance.

that getting old would make them forgetful, and so they became that stereotype.

This was not a one-off study. Researchers have replicated it time and again. Another study[16] includes the phrase "negative stereotypes, not facts, do the damage" as part of its title. The group conducting this research found that those who focus on the health challenges of aging often come to believe that declining health is inevitable. Thus they do nothing to promote good health and become less healthy than those who believe they have control of their health. Researchers have also found that people who accept the most depressing cultural images of old age live an average of 7.5 years less than those who are more optimistic.[17]

We could go on citing study after study, but we think we've made our point: If you are constantly told that retirement means spending your days playing shuffleboard while FaceTiming the grandkids, science says you are likely to fall into a stereotypical, boring, and possibly life-shortening retirement.

So what's a person to do if they want to avoid the stereotype threat? Change the model! The past does not need to be prologue. We can change the narrative and create a new model for "retirement." It's actually an anti-retirement model since it is the opposite of the current stereotype.

---

16   Lamont RA, Swift HJ, Abrams D, "A Review And Meta-Analysis of Age-Based Stereotype Threat: Negative Stereotypes, Not Facts, Do the Damage," *Psychology and Aging* 30, no. 1 (2015), 180–193, doi:10.1037/a0038586. https://pubmed.ncbi.nlm.nih.gov/25621742/.

17   Levy BR, Slade MD, Kunkel SR, Kasl SV, "Longevity Increased by Positive Self-Perceptions of Aging," *Journal of Personality and Social Psychology* 83, no. 2 (2002), 261–270, doi:10.1037//0022-3514.83.2.261, https://pubmed.ncbi.nlm.nih.gov/12150226/.

VIVA THE ANTI-RETIREMENT REVOLUTION!

Each generation's responsibility is to serve as a role model for the generations to come. For quite a few years, the work and retirement model was pretty set in stone. Men went to work wearing suits and ties. Women worked in administrative roles until they married and then stayed home with the children. When it was time to retire, they both settled quietly into a life of grandchildren, bridge games, and book clubs. Grandchildren would be encouraged to ask the oldsters what life was like "when you were young." It was assumed the grandparents would want to talk about the good ol' days because they saw that as the best part of their lives.

Well, the generation approaching or recently entering "retirement" has worked the past thirty or forty years to change just about every stereotype out there. As mentioned in the beginning of this book, we've driven and lived through the women's movement. We've embraced a flattening in hierarchal structures and a loosening of dress codes. Advancements in technology have changed work processes and outputs in ways that were unthinkable just a few years earlier. The generations entering the workforce today are walking into a completely different landscape from the one we first entered.

We want to create a model of retirement where the only stereotype is that there is none.

Now it's time to change the retirement model the way we changed the career model. We no longer want to fall into an outmoded stereotype. We want to create a model of retirement where the only stereotype is that there is none.

In the past you worked and were energetic, confident, and engaged. Then you retired, and you immediately became irrelevant.

People talked about becoming invisible. There is no reason for that to happen. Life is better viewed as one, long continuum where you gain knowledge, confidence, and new skills with every year, beginning in childhood and continuing throughout your life. There is no reason for a huge demarcation line between your working life and your post-working life. Yet stereotypes are hard to change. There needs to be a critical mass of people living an anti-retirement life to create a new vision of the postcareer phase and serve as role models for the next generations. We call those people "Resolutionists" because they have resolved to embrace the resolutions in this book and live life their way.

BECOMING A RESOLUTIONIST ROLE MODEL

It is hard to become a role model if no one knows who you are. So we have made it a priority to reach out to and build relationships with people of all ages. As we were going through our careers, we often skewed older in friends because they were the models and mentors we used to help guide our career decisions. We were all kindred spirits.

PATTI

Milledge and I have been modeling a very different "retirement" for my son and his husband than I had growing up. My parents and grandparents fell into the stereotypical retirement of golf games and church bazaars. They stopped learning and growing. They spent much of their time doing things that they had done for years. We have been much more dedicated to actively venturing outside our comfort zone. However, we always feel we can do better, so we asked our sons what things we did that drove them crazy. After their initial shock, they said, "You two are so active, you never rest. If you say, 'Hey do you want to go see a movie?' and we say yes, then you tell us that we have to walk three miles to get to the movie and then walk back." They love the fact that we stay healthy. But they had expected at this stage of life we would dial it down a notch and that their visits to us would be more restful. And we didn't let that happen. I suspect that when they get to our age, they won't be dialing it down a notch, either, because we are modeling a different type of retirement.

Now we are looking to influence up and down the age continuum, as well as within our age group—after all, being a Resolutionist isn't about age; it is about stage of life. Role modeling, at its core, is living your life in a way that others will find aspirational and will seek to emulate.

Our goal is to make "retirement" a more normal and desired state. We hope to help usher in a day when someone entering the workforce for the first time doesn't think about their life ending at retirement. We long for a time when financial planners and insurance companies don't divide your life into preretirement and postretirement phases. Becoming a Resolutionist does not mean turning into a totally different person. If you were high energy, interested in learning, willing to challenge yourself, and always setting and meeting goals during your career, why not continue that after your career?

Examples of high-profile Resolutionists who are using the post-career stage to continue to make huge impacts are all around us. Bill Gates is well known for the foundation he runs and its work on alleviating poverty. Jimmy Carter is well known for teaching in his local Sunday school, working on Habitat for Humanity projects, and heading international conflict resolution and election observation missions through the Carter Center. Mr. Gates and President Carter are both bigger-than-life role models that are leading the way, but we can all be part of the movement in our small part of the world.

The new anti-retirement model confirms that you aren't defined by your profession. Going back a few chapters to the elevator pitch resolution, you saw several examples that prove it is becoming much more common to leave your primary career and pick up something just as impactful in later life. You can—and probably will—have multiple dimensions to your life.

ACT YOUR AGE

How many times have you heard the phrase "Act your age!"? Whether said to a child or an adult, it typically means you are acting outside the "stereotype." When said to someone in "retirement," it normally means to stop being so foolish. It's time to slow down, sit back, relax—stop thinking you can compete with the younger generations.

MILLEDGE

The theme that runs through the anti-retirement movement is choice. Everyone should be able to choose the life that works for them, without judgment from others. However, that can be easier said than done. Patti and I had a goal one year to communicate with Dustin in the format that he prefers (text), not our preference (phone or email). He and I were soon texting all the time. When Patti and I reviewed our goals part way through the year, I proudly said how well the change in communication was working. And I followed that up with asking her how she thought the communication with Dustin was going. She also thought that it was going great since Dustin was communicating in the manner that he wanted (text) with whom he wanted to communicate (me). After laughing about her answer, I realized that we had achieved the goal and that she had outsmarted me again.

If you are part of the anti-retirement movement, it is important that you change this mindset. The movements over the past thirty years have focused on dramatically expanding choices. Men and women have become equal partners in supporting and raising a family, opening the career choices for both of them. Technology has changed how and where we work, making our work environments much more personal and flexible. Rigid social mores dictating "appropriate" behavior, clothing, and career choices have been smashed. We broke through stereotypical constraints in every facet of life. There is no reason this expansion of choices needs to stop now that we have stepped away from our careers.

As a Resolutionist, vow to break stereotypes and expand your list of possible activities in ways that are not defined by age or historic expectations. You can learn to fly fish or hip-hop dance; you can cruise around the world or kite surf at your local lake. The list is endless.

Don't convince yourself that you are destined to a life of watching evening game shows and baking pies (unless that is what you love to do). Nothing is off limits, so reach for the stars. Look forward rather than backward, and embrace the new you!

So, act our age? We *are* acting our age!

THIS IS OUR LIFE

It is not the strongest of the species that survives, nor the most intelligent; it is the one most adaptable to change.

—Charles Darwin

MUCH OF OUR thinking about "retirement" has been formed by the lives we've led. We are two very average people who have worked hard and are fortunate to now be in the *best* phase of our lives. However, though we are now in the same place, we got here along very different paths. We grew up in different parts of the country, in different social classes, and in different types of families. We've seen our share of ups and downs. Yet, despite our differences, we've found that the resolutions in this book work for both of us, as well as others. They are universal, whether you are chairman of an investment bank or the local librarian, whether you are CEO of a tech company or a graphic designer. When it comes time to step away from work, we are all the same. We are all looking for how to make the next two or three decades the best ever.

MILLEDGE

When I "retired," I knew I wanted more out of life than just running, reading, traveling, and playing golf. While

I thoroughly enjoyed increased travel and meaningful time with friends, I knew that I needed to contribute to the betterment of the world. When I was invited to join the board of Soles4Souls, I knew I had found the passion that would underpin all the other things I did for the foreseeable future. Soles4Souls turns shoes and clothes into opportunity by keeping them from going to waste and putting them to good use creating jobs and providing relief. Its mission is to eradicate poverty. I really became hooked when I traveled with the group to hand out the shoes in Honduras. It felt like a million degrees outside, and I was whining about the heat. Then these children showed up, barefoot and mud-caked because they didn't have shoes or clean clothes, and they couldn't have been happier. We washed their feet and fitted each kid with a new pair of shoes until we ran out. This experience had a huge impact and helped me consider all of the blessings given to me. It was the vehicle I had been looking for to really make a difference. To me, this is what living a Resolutionist life is all about.

People will often say, "Wow, you two are so lucky to have the jobs and life you did!" But we all make our own luck. We worked hard to get where we are. Patti was the only one of her siblings to attend college and was willing to leave her small Midwestern hometown to follow her dreams. Milledge too forged his own path separate from his family.

Despite our differences and the different paths we've taken, we share a common set of values. And those are values that work no matter where you are in life. One of our most important characteristics is adaptability. When life knocked us off kilter, we simply refocused and determined our best path forward. We've changed and adapted as the environment around us has changed. Even now, in what would typically be a more stable time of life, we have seen some of our goals upended by the COVID-19 pandemic. Life simply isn't the way we had planned it. The seismic changes brought about by the pandemic are bringing our innate adaptability front and center again, as well as proving that the resolutions we have adopted can provide stability in all types of climates.

In fact, the pandemic has turned out to be a microcosm of this book.

The shelter-at-home orders have been a rip-the-Band-Aid-off moment. One day we were planning a monthslong trip, and the next day we were stockpiling face masks and hand sanitizer. We had to set goals that we could accomplish from home and develop metrics to fit our new reality.

We had to find a way to get comfortable with the uncomfortable. We all had lots of questions, but there were no answers. We had to find ways to do things differently. We definitely had to learn how to be our own best friend because we were the only ones in our shelter. Reaching friends and loved ones in new and different ways and sharing our lives virtually became the new normal.

And we had to do all of this with FOMO whispering in our ears that there were things happening out in the world that we couldn't be part of.

It really brought home that the Resolutionist mindset is about being adaptable. The fact is that "the only constant in life is change." The twelve resolutions can help you adjust to the change. They work for anyone wanting to make their life more fulfilling and happy, whether in a pandemic or in more "normal" times. In fact, most of them would also work for people still in the midst of their career who need a framework to help them adapt to a changing environment.

These are tools that can be purposed and repurposed. If someone plans a major undertaking but then gets sick, they can simply fall back on the Resolutionist strategy to adapt and make new goals. In the middle of a pandemic, we can use the resolutions to reexamine earlier decisions and see if they are still right given our new reality.

The Resolutionist life is for anyone and everyone who wants to fully live their life, from beginning to end. No bending to social norms, no creating a false demarcation between working and not, and no acting our age. We are two people reimagining what is possible at this stage of life that has traditionally been thought of as "retirement." We have stepped back from our careers but not from living. Become a Resolutionist and join us on our journey. We sincerely believe the best is yet to come.

ABOUT THE AUTHORS

PATTI S. HART

Patti Hart spent her early life in a small town in Illinois cheering for her Chicago Cubs, going to public schools, and sharing chores with her many siblings. Her role models were in the most unlikely places—her high school teacher who pushed for organized girls sports and won; her grandmother, a woman ahead of her time in strength and resolve; and her guitar instructor, who was unafraid to take center stage in a business dominated by men. Though life was not always easy, it was filled with laughter, hugs, support, and challenges.

Patti was fortunate to find her way into the telecommunications industry at a time when no one could have predicted the growth and change that lay ahead. Several promotions and numerous relocations later, she found herself in places she never thought she would go. She took risks and defied the odds to enjoy a career that spanned three decades of leadership positions in the technology sector and was honored to be a member of *Fortune* magazine's inaugural list of "Most Powerful Women" in 1998.

Patti has worn many professional hats: CEO, chairman, board member, investor, and advisor, but is most proud of her personal life as wife, mother, sister, daughter, neighbor, and friend. As an adult, she has called many cities home and found each place to offer wonderful opportunities to learn and grow.

She has always valued community involvement and has dedicated her free time to advancing the arts, human rights, and "sport for all."

Patti is a proud alumna of Illinois State University and counts herself as a lifetime "Redbird." She was named ISU's Distinguished Alumna in 2015.

In her "retired but engaged" stage of life, this Resolutionist splits her time between the beauty of Lake Tahoe and the intellect of Silicon Valley.

MILLEDGE A. HART

Milledge Hart is a native of Dallas, where playing high school football and becoming an Eagle Scout were expected. Milledge began his overachievement early, becoming an Eagle Scout before the age of fifteen and having his godfather, Ross Perot, present him with the medal commemorating his accomplishment.

Milledge was blessed with many gifts in life. His father, Mitch Hart, gave him the gift of "not being afraid to set the bar high." His grandmother gave him the gift of respecting discipline and the benefits of a regimented life. And Duke University gave him the gift of an education far beyond the classroom, where he began to realize what was possible.

Following his collegiate years, Milledge moved to two new worlds—New York City and investment banking. Both would later become foundational parts of his future. The next step in his journey was to gain operational experience. A better understanding of his clients was eye-opening and would prove to be valuable as he made his way to California to, ultimately, form a new investment bank with several partners. But this time he could approach his work with his clients' priorities in mind.

Milledge credits much of his success to the advice and counsel he received from others and chose, through his leadership at the Entrepreneurs' Organization and involvement with the Young Presidents' Organization, to "pay it forward."

Personally, Milledge had never seen himself becoming a parent, but as we know, life is full of surprises! He has embraced his role as one of the many parents to Patti's son and has found it to be one of the most challenging but most rewarding parts of his life.

As a newly minted Resolutionist, Milledge enjoys the diversity of his portfolio: working through charitable organizations to make the world a better place while still advancing corporate activities in a variety of industries.

Printed in the USA
CPSIA information can be obtained
at www.ICGtesting.com
JSHW012050140824
68134JS00035B/3354